25

LIFE-CHANGING QUESTIONS

FROM THE GOSPELS

"An excellent book written clearly and succinctly by a skilled and inspiring teacher and author. *25 Life-Changing Questions from the Gospels* is an invitation to examine and critically evaluate life's big questions. It is a good exercise for everybody to consider in their spiritual journey and discipleship. Take up and read!"

Ines Murzaku
Professor and Founding Chair of the Department of Catholic Studies
Seton Hall University

"As a spiritual director, it becomes evident in the spiritual life that it is not sufficient to talk *about* Jesus, but rather, we must come to know him personally in dialogue with him. In this lucid and accessible work, Allan Wright opens a path to that conversation by allowing us to meet Jesus intimately as our Lord asks the key questions about life and faith to each one of us directly. *25 Life-Changing Questions from the Gospels* is such a help to deepening this intimate bond with our Lord!"

Msgr. Joseph R. Chapel
Spiritual Director
Casa Santa Maria, Pontifical North American College, Rome

"Whether teaching the parables of Jesus or leading retreats and workshops, Allan Wright powerfully engages audiences with the Word of God, launching and accompanying them on a spiritual journey of self-reflection and soul-searching. This gift for inspirational teaching also shines through in *25 Life-Changing Questions from the Gospels* where Allan invites us to hear Christ gently questioning us and beckoning us to draw nearer to Divine love. Unpacking these questions, Allan gives us the tools to respond authentically to Christ's invitation as we embark not only on a journey but also on a Divine transformative adventure."

Dianne M. Traflet
Associate Dean for Graduate Studies and Administration
Immaculate Conception Seminary

"I've seen many books that answer people's questions about Jesus, but this is the first one I've seen that asks people to answer Jesus' questions about them. Whether you're a life-long believer or a just curious about Christianity, this book can help you meet Jesus as if for the first time."

John Bergsma
Author of *Bible Basics for Catholics*

25

LIFE-CHANGING QUESTIONS

FROM THE GOSPELS

Letting Jesus Lead You through the
Stages of Spiritual Growth

ALLAN F. WRIGHT

AVE MARIA PRESS AVE Notre Dame, Indiana

Founded in 1865, Ave Maria Press is a ministry of the United States Province of Holy Cross.

www.avemariapress.com

Paperback: ISBN-13 978-1-59471-675-1

E-book: ISBN-13 978-1-59471-676-8

Cover design by Angela Moody, amoodycover.com.

Text design by Katherine J. Ross.

Printed and bound in the United States of America.

Library of Congress Cataloging-in-Publication Data is available.

Lauder Deo Mariaeque

To my wife, Desiree,
a constant source of love, faith, and encouragement,
and our four children: Sophia, Cataleen, Abigail, and Joseph
Joy upon joy upon joy upon joy!

Quaerite primum regnum Dei

CONTENTS

PREFACE

As a teacher for close to thirty years, I have come to realize that good teachers provide good answers, but exceptional teachers ask great questions. Isn't it true that such questions force the listener to wrestle with life's challenges and complexities? At times, questions can prompt those who hear them to rethink their assumptions and even reconsider the courses of their lives. There is no greater teacher than Jesus Christ, and it's evident from the four gospels that Jesus asked many simple yet profound questions that continue to challenge, inspire, and resonate within the human heart.

Why focus on questions as a spiritual journey? It has been my experience that critical thinking is not driven by answers, but by questions. Profound questions drive our thoughts beneath the surface of what may seem routine and force us to deal with some of life's challenges. Questions of purpose force us to define our tasks. Questions of interpretation invite us to examine how we are organizing or giving meaning to information. Questions of assumption compel us to examine what we are taking for granted. Questions of implication help us to consider where our thinking is going to lead us. Questions regarding point-of-view drive us to examine our ideas and to consider other relevant perspectives, including God's view, as revealed in sacred scripture.

Throughout the four gospels, Jesus asks well over one hundred questions. I have selected twenty-five of these, divided into five categories along the stages of a spiritual journey. Throughout these pages, we will cover the context, background, and setting of each question and then reflect on how the question can assist us in progressing along our own spiritual journey. Our journey begins with a spiritual curiosity about God and the person of Jesus. From there, we can begin lifelong discipleship in communion with the Body of Christ, the Church.

I've written this book for those seeking more in life who may never have considered Jesus, as well as for Christians who wish to be challenged further in their own faith—to be agitated, if you will, by Jesus' questions. It is my hope that Jesus' questions will arouse curiosity and prompt readers to delve into God's word, that some will be drawn from complacency and moved outside their comfort zones. I have a special interest in those who have been inoculated to the faith. By inoculated, I mean those who have gone through a program in the Church or school yet have never truly experienced or encountered the love of Jesus in a meaningful, personal way. If you are one of those readers, may this book enable you to look again at Jesus through *fresh eyes*.

Allan F. Wright
Feast of St. Joseph, Patron of the Universal Church

ACKNOWLEDGMENTS

I'd like to thank my wife, Desiree, for helping to keep order and sanity in our home during my late-night writing and for modeling the love of God in all she does. I'm also grateful to our children: Sophia, Cataleen, Abigail, and Joseph, whose joy and laughter brings life to our lives and reminds us that the best way to serve the Church is to live the Faith in our home.

To my mother, Jane Wright, who has modeled a life of faithfulness to Jesus and his church, and to the memory of my father, Ivan, whose humor, wisdom, and mannerisms I appreciate more and more each day: thank you.

My sincere thanks to the Missionaries of Charity-Contemplative Order, in particular those sisters in formation in Plainfield, New Jersey, whose witness to the love of Jesus continues to inspire my family and me—and no doubt to help satiate the thirst of Jesus for souls.

I extend gratitude to various "old timey" New Jersey diners such as the Summit, the Crossroads, the Tick Tock, the Victoria, and other Silk City and Kullman masterpieces where I have sought inspiration and respite at the counter over a ham-and-cheese omelet, home fries, white toast, and coffee.

To those who work faithfully at St. Paul Inside the Walls, the Catholic Center for Evangelization in the Diocese of

Paterson, New Jersey: thank you for giving life and expression to the New Evangelization under the leadership of Bishop Arthur J. Serratelli and Fr. Paul Manning. In grateful thanksgiving for the wisdom of Julie Burkey and Dianne Traflet who always have an encouraging word for me or a keen spiritual insight that they convey with ease and joy.

I offer grateful appreciation to Amber Dolle for taking time to "look things over" and for sharing her trusted perspective. Lastly, many thanks for the guidance of Kristi McDonald, whose suggestions and encouraging words enabled this project to get off the ground.

ONE

Away from the Numbers

1

WHAT ARE
YOU LOOKING FOR?

John 1:38

It is Socrates who is credited with the maxim, "The unexamined life is not worth living." In our ever-changing world, so full of complexity and uncertainty, there remains the inclination *not* to examine our lives too closely for too long. Living life without self-reflection seems, perhaps, an easier path to take. We can easily tune in to the voices of our culture, voices that scream at us to conform to the latest fad and, in doing so, set aside any hope of self-examination. Whether it's the latest message that pops up on our social media feed, the chatter of the twenty-four-hour news cycle, or the chaos of managing a busy household, there are plenty of distractions that keep us from pondering life's *big questions*.

Aside from the distractions, we have the task of sifting through all those "answers" that are so readily provided for our problems. Other people are quick to assure us that we are on the right path—that is, if it is *their* path. These voices offer simple directions and step-by-step instructions on how to think and how to act: study hard, attend a good college, build your resume, network your way up the corporate ladder, work long hours, be politically correct, never tolerate intolerance, and then work even harder and put in longer hours. Whew! While there is nothing inherently evil or intrinsically wrong with education, finances, investments, and hard work, is that the road that leads to joy? Is that all there is? Aren't we made for something more?

The examined life takes some work. It requires time. It requires silence. It requires asking those big questions and having a heart, mind, and will open to the answers. *What is my purpose? Why am I here?* The examined life also involves courage. For in asking the big questions and discerning the answers through study, humility, counsel, and receptive hearts and minds, we sometimes find answers we don't really like. We may be called to alter our courses in life, to relinquish control of those ever-perfect plans we've created. We may be called to embrace change, which is never easy for it may involve risk.

The first words out of the mouth of Jesus in the Gospel of John form a question: "What are you looking for?" Jesus poses this question to two disciples of John the Baptist. John observes Jesus walking by and calls out, "Behold, the Lamb of God" (Jn 1:36). That's a strange way to identify someone, yet the title provides insight into who John the Baptist believes Jesus is. John uses language of the Jewish Passover to describe Jesus' ultimate purpose. The two disciples must be intrigued by their master's identification of Jesus as the sacrificial "Lamb of God" because they immediately begin to follow Jesus. John the Baptist has a definite idea of Jesus' identity, and he is not afraid to verbalize it. It is John who points to Jesus, yet these followers must decide for themselves who they believe this man truly is. Often, our journey begins by another person pointing the way, calling something or someone to our attention, or simply living life in such a way that we aim to emulate. However, we have to personally make that decision to change our lives; it cannot be made for us.

What Are You Looking For?

Jesus poses this rather straightforward question to the two disciples. It is a simple yet complex one for them to consider; it is a simple yet complex one for *us* to consider some two thousand years later. In contemplating the question, we might be able to dive below the surface of our daily routines and seek our heart's true desires.

Having an answer for life's questions is a good thing. Having answers that make sense and connect us to something bigger than ourselves is better. Doing the interior work and arriving at truth in order to find the answer is perhaps the best.

I vividly remember sitting in my Algebra II class in high school and not having a clue what "X" was or how to solve for it. The teacher sat us alphabetically, and by chance, there was a brilliant, Russian foreign exchange student who sat right behind me. Let's just say that on more than one occasion, my head turned a full 180 degrees to "stretch" and cast my eyes upon his answer. That answer was quickly placed in the appropriate blank space on my paper. Unfortunately (or fortunately for me), I had one of those teachers who wanted more than the answer. He demanded that we show the work. *What were the steps that led you to the answer? . . . Show the work!* It was difficult, and it did take more time, but the end result was not only the correct answer but also a sense of accomplishment in knowing that this answer had not come freely.

In responding to our Lord's question, "What are you looking for?" it is appropriate to take some time to reflect on our own circumstances, behaviors, and attitudes. Taking time to analyze our own lives can lead us to think about the risks of our current behaviors and attitudes and begin to articulate what we are indeed seeking in this life. It's also prudent to take a critical view of how we have lived our lives up to this point, for what we believe is important may not be reflected in the decisions and life choices we've made. For example, if we claim that our health is important to us but we never exercise and we spend our days eating junk food, then our desire to be healthy is not reflected in our reality. It is also important to process the innumerable messages that our culture provides on a daily basis, communicating to us in obvious and subtle ways what is important in life. According to our society, being popular, wealthy, and famous as well as fitting in, standing out, and being outrageous provide happiness and purpose in life. While not everything our popular culture sells us is evil, it must all be examined in light of what is true, beautiful, and good. Such analyzing, reflecting, and examining mark a few of the initial steps in doing the work to get to an answer.

In response to the question that Jesus poses to the two disciples, they ask, "Where are you staying?" (Jn 1:38). In today's language, this is equivalent to asking, "May I be your student?" To be a disciple means to be disciplined and devoted, absorbing everything about the one giving instruction. In the pages of the Bible and in Rabbinic commentary, we often find the phrases, "sitting at the feet," or "wearing out the door" of the one who instructs. These are both ways of communicating that one is learning from a master.

John the Baptist, who has disciples of his own, recognizes that there is something special about Jesus and points his disciples toward him. They are curious about this relatively young rabbi and decide to take the next steps and spend time with this person to understand more about him—thus the question about where he is staying.

Jesus replies by saying, "Come, and you will see" (Jn 1:39). His response to their inquiry is spontaneous, brief, and beautiful. An invitation with a promise is given, and their journey begins.

"What are you looking for?"

PRAY

God, I'm looking for more from this life. I'm not quite sure if you're real, where you fit in, or even exactly where I should begin to seek and find you. Accept this prayer as a first step in my journey. Guide my steps as I ask the bigger questions of life, and give me openness to what may be out there for me. Help me to use my mind to critically examine what is true, and let me see a sign or two that I'm on the right path. Amen.

CONTEMPLATE

"Deep within his conscience man discovers a law which he has not laid upon himself but which he must obey. Its voice, ever calling him to love and to do what is good and to avoid evil, sounds in his heart at the right moment. . . . For man has in his heart a law inscribed by God. . . . His conscience is man's most secret core and his sanctuary. There he is alone with God whose voice echoes in his depths."

Catechism of the Catholic Church, 1776

WONDER

1. What is your initial response to the question, "What are you looking for?"
2. Have you ever been misguided by thinking that something or someone was the final answer to the purpose of life? If so, what happened?
3. When is the last time you took time alone to think about life and where you're going?
4. What may be some next steps for you in your spiritual journey?

2

WHAT IS YOUR NAME?

Luke 8:30

The most important word in real estate is *location*. The most important word in searching for truth, meaning, and joy in life is *relationship*. Human beings have a desire to know the truth and be connected to another person, not merely to an idea or a philosophy. In chapter 8 of the Gospel of Luke, we read about Jesus and his small band of followers as they travel throughout the northern part of Israel called Galilee. What they experience and whom they encounter will certainly shake the disciples up, but it will also reveal to them in part who is this Jesus that they are beginning to follow.

Jesus enters a boat with his disciples and says, "Let us cross to the other side of the lake" (Lk 8:22). The reader might be tempted to think that the "other side" is merely an indication of where the disciples are heading, a directional detail. In Jesus' day, however, the phrase, "the other side" had other implications apart from directional. The "other side" was the non-Jewish side, the Gentile side where Jewish religious law was neither observed nor practiced. Twenty-seven Jewish villages are mentioned in the gospels. With the exception of Jerusalem, they are each small and nondescript. Jesus is never recorded as entering a non-Jewish town, and it would be safe to assume that the disciples had never stepped foot on the "other side" before they met Jesus. The Gentile side would have had non-kosher foods, graven images, theaters in which Greek and Roman gods were glorified, and a host of other cultural practices that would have made it difficult, if not impossible, for a faithful Jew to abide by the Law.

The disciples, who are at the initial stages of following Jesus, make a decision to step into the boat with him as he sets forth to sail to the other side. We can imagine the anxiety and trepidation these men experience as they start to trust Jesus, a young rabbi, and begin the voyage not knowing what to expect. However, traveling with Jesus proves more eventful than they could have imagined because in the midst of their short four mile journey, the unanticipated but not infrequent occurs. A violent windstorm sweeps down upon this body of water.

The Sea of Galilee lies 680 feet below sea level. It is surrounded by hills, especially on the east side where they reach in excess of two thousand feet high. These heights are a source of cool, dry desert air. In contrast, the climate on the water and shore is almost tropical, with warm, moist air. The great difference in height between surrounding land and the sea causes large temperature and pressure changes, resulting in strong winds funneling through the hills and sweeping down upon the sea. The Sea of Galilee is somewhat small, and these winds may descend directly to the center of the lake, with violent results. When the contrasting air pressures meet, a storm can arise quickly and without warning. Small boats caught out on the sea are in immediate danger; such is the case, as we read in this story, where the water is relatively shallow, only two hundred feet at its greatest depth.

During this violent storm, Jesus is asleep in the boat. The disciples are terrified and awaken him, crying out, "Master! Master! We are perishing!" (Lk 8:24). Jesus arises, he rebukes the wind and the waves, and they subside.

As the disciples step onto solid ground on the other side, we can only imagine the looks they exchange between themselves, perhaps expressing: "What have we gotten ourselves into?" and "Who is this man?" At that moment, as the disciples are pulling the boat ashore, they are confronted by a demon-possessed man wearing no clothes, who lives among the tombs. We read that iron chains and shackles couldn't contain him. It's easy to imagine the disciples walking slowly backwards, eager to get back into the boat and return to the "safe" side of the lake.

The man's shocking appearance and possession by demonic spirits doesn't deter Jesus from moving forward. While the disciples no doubt stare in wonder at the scene unfolding before their eyes, Jesus approaches and asks a question: "What is your name?" (Lk 8:30).

What Is Your Name?

Exchanging names is the beginning of relationship. We are known by our names. Names can carry the weight of our ancestry for good or bad, and throughout the Bible, names not only designate a person's identity, region, and family, but they also suggest the traits of the person. Knowing someone's name empowers others because it carries with it an aspect of familiarity that implies they not only know who a person is but that they have some power over them.

The answer given to Jesus' simple, relational, and straightforward question is alarming. It reveals not the man's name but, rather, his condition. His parents didn't name him "Legion," but the many demons who possess him identify themselves as such. This man is certainly to be pitied because he can't articulate his own name; he doesn't know who he is. In the presence of Jesus, the demons take flight, and we later find the man, once possessed, sitting at Jesus' feet, fully clothed and in his right mind.

We can only speculate as to what the disciples are thinking as this scene plays out before them. *Who is this man? The wind and waves obey him; those possessed by demons are set free from their affliction.*

Jesus' question, "What is your name?" allows us to change places with the once-possessed man and cast aside any preconceived notions we might have about Jesus or what we've heard about him through others. Jesus is not too concerned nor taken aback with the outward appearance of the man, his history in the village, his lack of status in the community. He sees beyond all these things and beyond his affliction. For us, Jesus' question has the ability to strip aside how we are defined by others and even how we may present ourselves before him.

We may have advanced degrees, drive expensive cars, and present ourselves as successful to the world, but at our cores, what are the names by which we define ourselves? We may live in poverty, have a history of poor decisions, and in the eyes of others, be a lost cause. Do we let the past define us when we stand before Jesus? Is it enough to stand in front of Jesus and introduce ourselves without any of our accomplishments, failures, excuses, or afflictions and begin to get to know him for ourselves and allow ourselves to grow in knowledge of him? Jesus affirms us as his children, created in the image and likeness of God. Our value in his eyes never changes. In freedom, Jesus comes to meet you and me and calls us "friend," as he did with Lazarus and even Judas.

The disciples, Jesus' inner circle, started this journey in a boat in the midst of a storm and were beginning to see more than a carpenter, more than a religious teacher. The challenge for everyone intrigued by Jesus is to see him with fresh eyes and hear his words anew, and then we can begin to introduce ourselves to him. Perhaps we will be open to continuing the journey, for knowing about someone is vastly different than *knowing* them. Remember, it's about relationship, relationship, relationship.

PRAY

Jesus, there are a lot of people who talk about you and claim to represent you. At times, I have no idea what is true or what to believe. More often than not, I'm skeptical. At times my life is like that boat on the sea, but unlike your followers, I don't always know where to turn or whom to turn to. Here I am; allow me to get to know you more. Amen.

CONTEMPLATE

"If you are what you should be, you will set the whole world ablaze!"

St. Catherine of Siena

WONDER

1. What is holding you back from standing before Jesus and introducing yourself to him?
2. What do you think of when you hear the name *Jesus*?

3. Do you hide behind reputation, status, affliction, or prestige rather than letting others see you for who you are?
   If so, why?
4. Is there anything holding you back from letting Jesus and
   other people see you? What might you need to work on
   in yourself in order to open up to Jesus?

3

DO YOU WANT TO BE WELL?

John 5:6

On the Eastern side of the ancient city of Jerusalem, near the Sheep Gate and close to the Fortress of Antonio, there are a number of ritual baths, or in Hebrew, *mikvehs*, in which the ritually "unclean" used to bathe before offering their sacrifices in the Temple. Two thousand years after the Gospel was written, little attention would have been given to one of these pools and its *living* water—one of these *mikvehs*—except that a man who had been ill for thirty-eight years encountered Jesus while hoping to be placed in that pool. The pool is known as the Pool of Bethesda, a word that literally means the house or place of mercy.

Until its discovery in the nineteenth century, there was no evidence outside John's gospel for the existence of this pool. Scholars and academics had argued that the gospel was written by someone without firsthand knowledge of the city of Jerusalem. In their minds, the pool had only a symbolic, rather than historical, significance. Yet archaeologists and tourists alike can confirm that this ancient pool exists and was operating even years before the birth of Jesus.

Archaeologists have excavated several snake figures at the pool, evidence that the expanse also accommodated an

Asclepeion, a pool dedicated to the Greek god of healing, Asclepius.[1]

One thing that we know today, of which the ancients were perhaps unaware, is that an underground system of small water channels and springs brought water to this pool. Invalids would wait by the pool in anticipation of the "miraculous" stirring of water in hopes of being made whole by the god Asclepius. The belief was that whoever was the first one in the "magic waters," stirred by the unseen springs, would be healed of ailments and would then regain access to family and society; they would be whole.

It is possible, then, that the blind, lame, and paralyzed people who gathered around this pool were not hoping for the God of Israel to heal them but, rather, the mythical god Asclepius. If this is true then there is a tension in the passage from St. John's gospel: Who are you going to believe can heal you, the "god" Asclepius or Jesus who claims to be God?

We, living in the twenty-first century, can look back with some pity at those who were ill and seeking a magical cure from a pool of water. Most people in the Western world have ample access to medical care and the latest drugs and procedures. While we might joke that our healthcare system is not much better than what these poor souls could access, we would not be found sitting near a pool waiting for its waters to stir, nor would we list "living water" as our primary care provider.

Do You Want to Be Well?

In the Gospel of St. John, Jesus approaches the sick man. He takes the initiative and asks him a question: "Do you want to be well?" Jesus is not afraid to draw near to a person who is ill and ask a straightforward question. I would say there could have been two possible answers, the first one being, "Yes! Of course I want to be well!" and the second, "No; I'm okay. My limited needs are met. Being healed will only make me face new responsibilities, so I'm fine." The sick man, however, gives a different answer to Jesus' simple yet profound question.

He replies, "Sir, I have no one to put me into the pool when the water is stirred up; while I'm on my way, someone else gets down there before me" (Jn 5:8).

Jesus again takes the initiative, saying to him, "Rise, take up your mat, and walk." We are told that immediately the man became well, took up his mat and walked (Jn 5:9).

This story made it into the pages of the New Testament. The eyewitnesses of this account were most likely awestruck. The oral and written tradition of Christianity affirms that it occurred, and the Church still reads this story and proclaims that it happened two thousand years later.

You might be able to say, "Okay, I wasn't there. I don't have scientific proof it happened. If it did happen, I'm happy for the sick man . . . but what does this story that took place two thousand years ago, in a foreign city and culture, have to do with me today?"

There are a number of comparisons that we can make with this story as it relates to life in the twenty-first century. *Do you want to be well?* Then I ask you: *What is your pool?* This man was ill and sought potential healing in a pool of water. What is *your* pool? What is it that you believe will give you wholeness and peace and joy, a joy that doesn't depend upon circumstances but remains constant despite the uncertainties of life? It seems we have all had those "pools" in life. In grade school, around Christmastime, we would say, "If I could only get this toy then life will be great!" We'd receive the toy, and the excitement would fade in a short period of time; then we'd be on to the next thing. In high school, we might have said to ourselves, "If only I could make the honor roll, if only I could make Varsity, if only I could get my license, if only that guy or girl would finally notice me, then life will be perfect!" We discovered that some other need always appeared in effort to satiate our hunger for joy, for peace, for love that no created thing or human person could fulfill. As we moved forward in life, the "if onlys" continued. "If only I could get that job or that promotion, if only my boss would get off my back, if only my kids would . . . then I'll be well."

Around the pool in John's gospel are the ill, blind, lame, and crippled, as well as this man who is apparently paralyzed. We may not think that we have too much in common with these folks around the pool, but maybe there are some similarities. For more than twenty years, I taught in a high school where I really enjoyed each and every day. It was a privilege to be involved in some small way in the lives of those young men and women as teacher, coach, and activity moderator. The students were wonderful. As much as I enjoyed them, I can honestly say that they weren't too different from those who sat around the pool of Bethesda.

Some of my students were blind: blind to the existence of God and blind to the fact that they were created in his image and likeness. Whatever God does, he does beautifully and perfectly, yet many failed to see that, and the consequences were evident. Some of my students were crippled: crippled by the cruel words spoken to them; crippled by unhealthy self-esteem; crippled from neglect; crippled from constantly failing to meet the expectations placed on them by parents, teachers, and coaches. A few of my students were paralyzed: afraid to let others know who they truly were—for if they let others know how they felt or how they viewed life, they would be excluded, isolated, and alone. If they were not the "class clown" for a day, or the "jock," or the "overachiever" but, instead, let others know who they really were, they might have been free; but they feared rejection, which kept them playing the roles.

Do you want to be well? What's your pool? What is it that you believe will bring you wholeness and joy? You don't need to be a Rhodes scholar to realize that money, popularity, and fame are not the answers. A brief look behind the scenes at the wealthy, famous, and popular reveals a brokenness, a wounded state, that is familiar to those who are seeking to be well. Does an increase in the use of drugs, legal and illegal, point to a desire to be well? Does living in a culture where relationships are transitory and males and females use each other speak of joy or fulfillment? Do various philosophies intrigue us yet leave us wanting in the inner core of our beings?

Whatever is your answer, go for it with full force and see if it satisfies the desires of your heart. That emptiness inside is due not to the lack of material things but it's a *felt* lack of grace due to sin. When we surrender to God's grace, he will give us the abundant life we desire.

Jesus comes to you and poses the same question he posed to a nameless man known only by his illness: "Do you want to be well?" Following Jesus will be difficult. It calls us to a new way of life with new responsibilities, but there is

wholeness. There is joy. There is love. There is purpose in
life when we begin to trust and follow.

PRAY

God, I do want to be well. I want something that lasts and
that will be worth any effort I put in. There are a lot of "pools"
out there in which some people seem to be enjoying themselves, yet I think I may be made for more. I want truth; I
want to be well. Amen.

CONTEMPLATE

"The Lord does not disappoint those who take this risk;
whenever we take a step towards Jesus, we come to realize
that he is already there, waiting for us with open arms."

Pope Francis

WONDER

1. What are some of the "pools" you've experienced in your
   life with regard to things that you thought would make
   you well?
2. Why didn't the sick man answer Jesus' question directly?
3. What are the implications of "being well"?

4

IF GOD SO CLOTHES THE GRASS OF THE FIELD, WHICH GROWS TODAY AND IS THROWN INTO THE OVEN TOMORROW, WILL HE NOT MUCH MORE PROVIDE FOR YOU, O YOU OF LITTLE FAITH?

Matthew 6:30

As parents of four children, my wife and I can attest to the fact that most of our time is spent providing one need or another for them. We are not waiting on our children hand and foot, aside from the baby, but we are helping them to journey through the world. As our young children navigate successfully through grade school and beyond, their needs may change, but there remains a desire to be provided for. When an issue arises in the family, it's usually because a need is not being met. At times, we must skillfully extract the "need" out of an older one, using the skills of a seasoned psychologist, while the toddler makes his needs known with a scream.

Being provided for does seem to be a basic need. Not that we should expect others to assume our responsibilities, but there is comfort in knowing that someone will be there, someone will be present for support even when everything else seems to be falling apart around us. Jesus calls his first disciples on the shore of Galilee, and they follow. These disciples then witness some miraculous cures and hear this young rabbi teach with authority like no one they've ever heard before. They are in the initial stages of their journey with him, and because of the huge crowds he's attracting, Jesus leads them up a mountain in order to teach.

The words Jesus speaks are recorded in what is referred to as the Sermon on the Mount. Some of the most memorable sayings of Jesus are found in this sermon, such as the Our Father and the Beatitudes, as well as the basis of expressions such as "turn the other cheek," "go the extra mile," and "stop judging others" (Mt 5:1–6:29e). As Jesus speaks, his disciples are both comforted and challenged.

In the Our Father, Jesus tells the crowd to pray for their daily bread, the bread of sustenance. For the faithful Jews, who are those gathered to hear Jesus speak on the mountain, the reference to daily bread is perhaps an allusion to the Old Testament story in which God provided bread, or *manna*, that came down from heaven daily in the wilderness. The manna miracle was intended to teach the Israelites to trust their God, who provided for their bodies and souls.

Jesus then tells them plainly not to store up treasures in this life but to store up treasures in heaven. Jesus continues speaking and proceeds to talk about trust, telling them plainly not to worry about tomorrow, about what to eat or drink or wear.

Jesus then turns his attention to the surrounding fields and fixes his gaze toward the rolling hills that abound in Galilee and are arrayed with beautiful flowers. The glorious

Yellow Asphodel, the radiant purple Khatamit Zifanit, the bright red Corn Poppy, the delicate Blue Lupine, and the lavender Pretty Carmelite, whose petite flowers blossom all the way to the coast of Haifa, blanket the terrain. It is here that Jesus, the master teacher, uses the visual beauty of his surroundings to make a point concerning trust. He says, "If God so clothes the grass of the field, which grows today and is thrown into the oven tomorrow, will he not much more provide for you, O you of little faith?" (Mt 6:30).

For those who have just heard Jesus' words, there is both comfort and a challenge. Comfort comes from knowing that God indeed clothes the grass and flowers of the field—and people are more valuable than grass and flowers. The challenge arises in the phrase, "O you of little faith." It's one thing to sit on a mountain, surrounded by rolling hills covered with flowers, and hear an animated speaker talk with authority; it's quite another to put those words into practice in the providence of your daily lives. It's the *putting into practice* that counts.

Up to this point, the disciples have seen some miraculous healings at the hands and words of Jesus, and this person they have left behind their fishing nets to follow is gaining popularity in the northern part of the country. We might imagine that these first followers think they are superior, being part of Jesus' "inner circle" and perhaps receiving special treatment. This is not the case, however. These first followers of Jesus will have to decide if they will stick with him. In speaking of God's provision for the birds of the air and flowers of the field, they will need to make a definite decision on who is this Jesus. He placates their fears with his words and calls them to trust God for their daily bread, to

turn the other cheek, and to follow many other new direc-
tives in his Sermon on the Mount. Jesus' words are indeed
powerful, but do his followers have the faith to continue the
journey? Does their initial curiosity wane when confronted
with the words, "O you of little faith"?

One of the references in the Sermon on the Mount mentions "our daily bread," as discussed earlier. If you recall
the miracle of manna recorded in Exodus, you know that
life for the Israelites was difficult, for they were in a land of
scarcity. When they had lived in Egypt, the Hebrews, like
the Egyptians, relied on the annual Nile River floods, which
provided rich soil for their food production, rather than the
unpredictable rainfall on which other countries relied. In
times of poverty, families went to Egypt. In Exodus, we find
the Israelites in the desert, far from water and rich soil.

When God provided the manna for the Israelites, they
began to hoard the food. When we don't know when our next
meal is coming or where it's coming from, the tendency is to
stockpile food. God gave the Israelites manna as his gift. As
it is recorded, the first thing they did when they saw bread
lying all over the ground was to grab as much of it as they
could because that's what they had done in Egypt whenever
there was a rare abundance of food. All of the manna that
they hoarded rotted by the next morning. They couldn't
use it at all. And so, over the course of the forty years, God
used this as a tool to teach the Israelites about trusting in
his providence. It was all about breaking the mindset of life
in Egypt, the mindset of slavery. The people learned they
couldn't hoard the manna; they could only take enough for
the day, which meant they had to start living by trusting in
God and learning to be generous with their neighbors. It was

easier for the Israelites to get out of Egypt than to get Egypt out of the Israelites.

When we experience periods of uncertainty and anxiety in our lives, we tend to do the same thing as the Israelites. Perhaps we don't build barns to store our hoarded food, but we tend to rely on ourselves and shut out others who may be a threat to our possessions.

If God So Clothes the Grass of the Field, Which Grows Today and Is Thrown into the Oven Tomorrow, Will He Not Much More Provide for You, O You of Little Faith?

God is indeed unpredictable, but he is never unfaithful. What fears might you have about letting go of an old way of life, an ingrained mode of thinking and acting, in order to embrace a new way of living that is in fact ancient in its origins: the life of faith in Jesus? We don't *detach* from one thing in life unless we intend to *attach* ourselves to another. The life of Christian faith is not a leap into the unknown but a step toward a person, a step to embrace Jesus and obedience to his way. There is no instant discipleship; there is no instant flower or fruit when a seed is planted. Our initial curiosity draws us closer to Jesus, and we find both an attraction to his compassion toward the sick and those on the margins of society and a comfort in his words. His words provide security in a manner that we may not have expected, for we are called to act on his words, which involves trust. As Christians, we may not know where we are going, but we do know who will accompany us.

PRAY

Jesus, your words are comforting and challenging. There is a lot of beauty in the world, but there is a lot of ugliness to go along with it. I feel as if I have left some of my "nets" behind like the first disciples, but I'm still searching. I'm open to hear more. Amen.

CONTEMPLATE

"I was in Penn Station at 7 a.m. before anyone else got there, and I was totally alone except for vendors. I had just gotten off the hour-long train ride that I took every morning and could feel the exhaustion in my shins from yesterday's hours of ballet. At eighteen years old I felt like I'd lived an entire lifetime. But in the belly of that empty station, I was a child. Out of nowhere from across the concourse, I heard the most beautiful music playing. There had been such a fierce emptiness growing in my heart lately, but the music filled me in a way that I knew only God could. I realized that he was everywhere. He filled the whole station; he filled everything. I knew that what he wanted was what I wanted, and there was hope in me for the first time. In acknowledging that hope, I felt as though I answered him, and I knew I had the protection of a Father."

Meghan Brulé

WONDER

1. Who has provided for you during your life? What type of security did that give you?

2. Recall a time when you stepped away from one situation of your own free will or were perhaps forced to venture into the unknown. What feelings accompanied that experience?
3. Do the words of Jesus bring comfort? If so, in what way?
4. Have you ever trusted Jesus by intentionally putting his words into practice? What happened?

5

DID YOU NEVER READ THE SCRIPTURES?

Matthew 21:42

St. Teresa of Calcutta once remarked that there are an awful lot of people who talk about prayer, but they never pray. In my experience, I would say the same is true when it comes to reading scripture. My sources for this include students in high school and college classrooms, groups at parish Bible studies, and people with whom I've had private conversations at parties. Inevitably, when the topic of the Bible comes up I'll hear people talk about their opinions of the scriptures. Even atheists, who can be quite vocal about their assurances that there is no God, become instant theologians and scripture scholars when the subject arises.

Perhaps the most common phrase I hear in relation to the scriptures is "Somewhere in the Bible it says . . ." Rarely, if ever, does a person cite the book, chapter, and verse, which would be extremely helpful in figuring out the context of what is being said. I know how I feel when my words are taken out of context or only half of what I said is quoted, and I imagine most people feel the same way. There will always be a few people with "anti-God" agendas who will pick and choose random verses in order to ridicule what they can't fathom, or those who won't make the effort to understand what the author attempts to communicate in his language and culture. (In Catholic theology, we call the study of interpretation and drawing out the meaning of the text *hermeneutics*.) At the other extreme are people who reduce the Bible to being God's "love letter" to us, which is a bit sentimental and not entirely accurate.

Even if approaching the scriptures from a skeptical or an atheistic perspective, there's enough historical and cultural significance—as well as drama, action, betrayal, and even sex—to keep a reader occupied for some time. For we who believe in Jesus, simply reading the Bible for information is not enough if we want it to have an impact on our lives. One of Jesus' apostles, St. James, offers some sound advice: "Be doers of the word and not hearers only, deluding yourselves. For if anyone is a hearer of the word and not a doer, he is like a man who looks at his own face in a mirror. He sees himself, then goes off and promptly forgets what he looked like" (Jas 1:22–24).

The Bible reveals one continuous story, from the first pages of Genesis to the last paragraphs of Revelation, the heart of which is relational. Some verses from Proverbs or Psalms work fine when read alone, but most scripture is meant to be understood in context, which, for the modern reader, takes some investigation. We can learn a lot more about a verse by examining the details surrounding it, such as who is its author, why was he writing, when was it written, what was going on historically at that time, and who was the recipient of the message. Most Bibles today offer some commentary at the bottom of each page, and many churches have a knowledgeable person or two who would jump at the chance to offer some assistance.

In a modern newspaper, there are different sections, each with its own form of language, jargon, and expression. One does not read the front page through the same lens as the comics or sports section. Context is important. If a person is murdered and it makes the front page, we assume a human life is lost, a family is devastated, and the police are involved in the investigation of a homicide. If the local baseball team gets "murdered" by the opposition, we don't call the police nor do we press charges against the victorious team who won by a wide margin. When we read the comics, we understand that humor is involved and the situations are satirical. If we see a talking cat in a comic strip, we don't call the publisher and accuse them of publishing lies because it's a scientific fact that cats can't speak English.

Did You Never Read the Scriptures?

As a person who has an advanced degree in scripture studies and who has benefitted from study in Jerusalem and taking courses in biblical Hebrew and Greek, I can say that my education has positively impacted my faith and my understanding of the Old and New Testaments that make up the Bible. However, when I first picked up a Bible to read it for myself, at around seventeen years of age, I didn't have any advanced degrees, ancient language knowledge, or scholarly insights. I was just curious to read the words of Jesus for myself. As a faithful churchgoer, I had heard the scriptures read for countless Sundays as a child, so I was familiar with a few things Jesus said, but I'd never had the opportunity to put the whole story together. Going to church was like receiving a few pieces of a jigsaw puzzle each week without seeing the big picture and knowing where they may fit.

When I did begin reading the gospels, there was something inside me that longed for more. I developed a hunger. As in the first stages of a romantic relationship, after the initial attraction, I desired to know more about what I read and about this Jesus who was central to the story. It was love seeking understanding.

The words of Jesus are accessible to peasants and scholars alike. The rabbis of Jesus' day were attracted to him, and the "Am haarez," the crowds of uneducated people, flocked to him as well. Jesus' longest-recorded sermon, the Sermon on the Mount (Mt 5–7), can be read in about seven minutes. His most well-known parable, the Good Samaritan, can be read in about thirty seconds and understood by a five-year-old. Jesus' parables are beautiful, basic, and brief stories that incorporate the life experience of the ordinary people among whom he lived. A man sowing seed, a woman sweeping the house in search of a coin, a man wanting fruit from a fig tree, a woman seeking justice from a corrupt judge, a man with a lost sheep, a woman sewing a garment, and a friend arriving at midnight are a few of the subjects of his parables.

In the four gospels, the accounts of Jesus written by four different authors, the word "home" is mentioned thirty times and the word "house" is mentioned ninety-nine times! So much of Jesus' healing, teaching, forgiving, and sharing meals takes place not in the scholastic centers of the day or in the Temple or synagogues but right in the homes where regular people live.[2] This is the living Word of God, which has the power to transform the lives of those who read it and are open to the message and person of Jesus.

G. K. Chesterton, a convert to Catholicism, writer, poet, and philosopher, among other things, wrote, "The poet only asks to get his head into the heavens. It is the logician who seeks to get the heavens into his head. And it is his head that splits."[3] This is a way of saying that the God revealed in the scriptures is mystery. This God who is mystery and more infinite than the human mind can conceive has revealed himself to us through Jesus. Do the scriptures reveal everything we may want to know about God? No. Do they reveal what we need to know for our salvation? Yes!

If you are serious about pursuing Jesus and leaving behind your mere curiosity about him to begin a new phase of considering who he is, then reading the scriptures is the next step. St. Jerome stated, "Ignorance of scripture is ignorance of Christ."[4] We can rely on others' opinions of who Jesus is, or we can get serious and go to his words directly.

PRAY

Jesus, I've heard a lot about you from others. Some people are sincere while others don't seem too genuine. I'm going to read your words for myself. If you have something to say to me, here I am. Amen.

CONTEMPLATE

"It is true that being a Christian means saying 'yes' to Jesus Christ, but let us remember that this 'yes' has two levels: it consists in surrendering to the Word of God and relying on it, but it also means, at a later stage, endeavoring to know better and better the profound meaning of this word."

St. John Paul II

WONDER

1. Have your words ever been misquoted or taken out of context? How did you feel?
2. Have you ever read the scriptures? Did you find them confusing or easy to understand?
3. How can learning about the context, background, and author assist in making sense of the scriptures?
4. What does it mean to read and study for information versus formation?

TWO

Nobody's Hero

6

DO YOU BELIEVE
THAT I CAN DO THIS?

Matthew 9:28

On February 22, 1980, the US Olympic ice hockey team pulled off one of the biggest upsets in sports history by defeating the mighty Soviet national hockey team in Lake Placid, New York. I can still hear the words of sportscaster Al Michaels as he marked the time with five seconds remaining and then exclaimed, with three seconds to go, *"Do you believe in miracles? Yes!"*

It was a defining moment in my childhood as a rabid hockey fan, and I still can't watch the video clip without getting emotional. It was a monumental victory and in a sense *miraculous*, for the chance that an amateur hockey team could defeat the Soviet Union's well-established professional team was one in a thousand. When we come across the word "miracle" in the Bible, however, we expect a little more than an improbable "miracle on ice."

We desire to know a little more information about the nature of the miraculous cure or changes that seem to contradict laws of physics. Our more advanced, more skeptical, and scientific minds demand additional evidence before we attach the word "miracle" to an event. It's true that even some Christian scholars shy away from the miracles of Jesus and are a little embarrassed by them. I've heard for myself and read articles in which people detract from the miracle stories and, with thinly veiled condescension, look down upon the *poor, uneducated* people of Jesus' day.

Early on in the gospels, we find out that one of the titles given to Jesus is that of miracle worker. The four gospels describe Jesus performing thirty-six specific miracles and mention that he performed even more during his three-year ministry. From healing people who suffered from skin diseases to restoring sight to the blind to even raising the dead, Jesus is recorded as having the ability to do the miraculous, and the gospel writers are not shy about including these miracles when telling their stories.

The New Testament contains several prominent stories involving people who are blind. Unlike modern definitions, which include people having some residual vision under the category of "legal blindness," the biblical languages all connote total and permanent loss of sight. Not all blind people in ancient times begged for a living; while many blind persons were undoubtedly poor, they lived like the majority of the people in the biblical world. Additionally, throughout ancient literature, the restoration of sight to blind persons is attributed only to the gods, so Jesus' healing ministry is distinctive.

When Jesus begins his public ministry in Capernaum, he enters their synagogue and is handed the scroll to read. He chooses the portion from the prophet Isaiah and reads, "The Spirit of the Lord is upon me, because he has anointed me to bring glad tidings to the poor. He has sent me to proclaim liberty to captives and recovery of sight to the blind, to let the oppressed go free, and to proclaim a year acceptable to the Lord" (Lk 4:18–19). Recovery of sight to the blind is one of the main objectives in the ministry of Jesus, and this can be seen both literally and figuratively.

In the story of the healing of the two blind men, Jesus is passing on from a village after healing a woman who had suffered from hemorrhaging and raising a little girl from the dead. News of these events has spread throughout the land, so even a blind person must have heard that there is a young rabbi who supposedly has the power to heal.

Two blind people follow Jesus as he is leaving town and cry out, "Son of David, have pity on us." It's interesting that even a blind person recognizes and discerns that there is something special about Jesus, albeit by reputation alone. They know their condition, which might seem obvious, but do we recognize our condition and need for Jesus? As we move closer to Jesus, we become more aware of who we are, including in our spiritual lives, and that there are areas in our lives that may need to change. Trying to change on our own is futile because we can't do it alone; we need the power that comes only from God.

What the blind men have heard about Jesus leads to action and they follow him. Being blind, they are assisted by others in their journey to Jesus. Jesus enters a house, and the blind men approach. Jesus takes the initiative and asks the question, "Do you believe that I can do this?" It's not recorded that the needs of the blind men were articulated or vocalized; perhaps it was just obvious. At other times Jesus has asked people what they needed. In this case, however, it is just known.

The men's response turns out to be both brief and beautiful. *"Yes, Lord."* These two blind men who first give Jesus the title, Son of David, respond to his question by calling Jesus "Lord." Perhaps these are words of desperation from men willing to say anything in order to be healed, yet Jesus responds with words that will affirm their authentic belief: "Let it be done to you according to your faith"(Mt 9:29). It would appear that their hearts were open and they were genuine in their belief in Jesus before their eyes were opened.

When these men were blind, they began to follow Jesus in hope. They had hope that he might provide something they desperately wanted; hope that their lives would be changed; hope that their eyes would be opened and a new way of life could be lived. Even though they didn't articulate their needs and desires, Jesus knew and took the initiative to ask the question. Such is the knowledge, love, and power of Jesus.

How about you? We all have desires that material things alone can't satisfy. Often we can't even express our desires because they're too deep or too personal for words, but we know that we've been created for something more. Do you have the "vision" of these blind men who recognized there was something more to Jesus than met the eye?

Do You Believe That I Can Do This?

The blind men whose sight Jesus restored couldn't contain themselves; they went out and spread the word about what had happened to them. This same Jesus meets you now; he meets you where you are and invites you into the same conversation, asking, "Do you believe I can do this?" Maybe you desire to have an encounter with Jesus. Maybe you wish to be free from past hurts, to be forgiven. Maybe you want to see yourself, others, and life differently and to begin to really live. Whatever it may be, are you open to begin to follow a little more closely and to trust?

PRAY

Jesus, I'm beginning to follow you, and I do have a few things that I would like you to do—although I'm not sure if it's more what I want or what you want. As you opened the eyes of blind men, please open my eyes to who you are. Amen.

CONTEMPLATE

"The wound in all of us, and which we are all trying to flee, can become the place of meeting with God and with brothers and sisters; it can become the place of ecstasy and of the eternal wedding feast. The loneliness and feelings of inferiority which we are running away from become the place of liberation and salvation."

Jean Vanier, founder of the L'Arche community and an untiring advocate for people with developmental disabilities

WONDER

1. What are the titles of Jesus that are most comforting or most challenging to you?
2. The blind men have hope and put their feet in motion to follow Jesus. How are you similar to the two blind men?
3. Do you believe that Jesus can identify your need and bring healing and wholeness?
4. Can you believe that God loves you for who you are and not for anything you have done? Why do you say that?

7

WHAT DO YOU WANT ME TO DO FOR YOU?

Matthew 20:32

There is an old saying that goes, "Be careful what you ask for because you just might get it." Part of me is thankful that I didn't receive everything I ever wished and prayed for as a child; if I had, there would be a big pony roaming around our small house as I type! It is fun to imagine ourselves answering open-ended questions, such as what we would do if we had unlimited wishes, power, money, and so forth. There is always the flipside, however, which involves those unforeseen and unintended consequences that can accompany wishes fulfilled. We might think that we'll handle the consequences and demands of being filthy rich because those must be better than being poor and out of the public eye. Just a quick glance at the "rich and famous" reveals that many who have these things have their issues and don't always seem joyful. The people who do whatever they want will get done what they never wanted to do, as the saying goes. It seems quite obvious that human beings can handle almost anything except perpetual prosperity.

What Do You Want Me to Do for You?

When Jesus asks the question, "What do you want me to do for you?" we should also tread cautiously, not because he is disingenuous, duplicitous, or misleading but because our answers will have consequences that we may not totally understand at first. As we learn more about Jesus, we will find that starting a relationship with him and following his way may not always be what we previously imagined. If it's only a "quick fix" to life's problems that we seek, Jesus is probably not the one to approach.

In the story that precedes the healing of the blind men, the mother of Sts. John and James approaches Jesus, pays him homage, and is about to present a request to him. Jesus anticipates her question and asks, "What do you wish?" Her request is bold and brazen: she asks for places of honor for her two sons. Perhaps she gives voice to the universal desire of mothers who wish success and honor for their children. Jesus basically tells her and her two sons, who are standing close by, that they have no idea what they are asking, for their idea of greatness in the kingdom of God is not in line with Jesus' view of greatness. They are following Jesus with their two feet, but they are selfishly thinking, "What's in it for me?" Their hearts and minds are not aligned to Jesus' way.

It's not uncommon for people to draw close to God in times of trouble and insecurity. We all need hope to sustain us in this uncertain world. All through the gospels, we find people attracted to Jesus and his message, drawing close to Jesus, fighting through the crowds in order to make their requests known to him. The mercy of God is on display in the person of Jesus as he reaches out, heals, comforts, allows himself to be touched, forgives, and gives life. While God desires that people are whole and that they experience joy and encounter his love through Jesus, there is a cost to following him. This is why today, as in Jesus' day, people walk away from him. The path to which he calls us is not easy. It's the way of love as defined by the Cross, but still, it's too difficult for many. Sts. James and John would later learn this.

Jesus is leaving Jericho where this time two blind men are sitting on the side of the road and crying out, "Son of David, have pity on us." The crowd warns them to be silent, but they call out all the more. Their desire to meet Jesus can't be diminished by the crowd.

It's at this moment that Jesus stops and calls to them, saying, "What do you want me to do for you?" They answer, "Lord, let our eyes be opened." Jesus touches their eyes, which are then opened, and they follow him. Sight has been restored, and these two blind men use their new sight to follow the one who can even make the blind see.

The question Jesus poses here is one that should cause us to reflect for a moment. Our initial answers may be enthusiastic responses to Jesus, voicing our needs; yet are we willing to follow the example of these two men whose sight was restored? Are we following Jesus because he is the way, the truth, and the life or because we believe that he is just here to serve us, to be at our beck and call, without any "skin in the game" on our parts? Our decisions, even if they are to stop our initial investigations of who Jesus is, will in no way diminish his love for us. It would go against his very nature to cease loving us. We even read in the gospels the story of ten lepers who were cured and only one who came back to give thanks. Jesus doesn't strike the nine who were healed with a new case of leprosy; he is not vengeful.

Are you taking this journey for a quick fix? An easy answer to life's dilemmas? A way to escape life by hiding in religion? If so, you should look elsewhere. Sts. James and John would soon find out that following Jesus leads to the cross, that dying to self is part of the equation, and that suffering, forgiving others, service, and mystery are involved, too.

The crowds today are not much different than crowds two thousand years ago. In fact, the crowds today are more vocal and use many voices and media outlets to discourage and advise against following this person Jesus, saying his name, or listening to the Church he founded. Is this the path you want to take? Will you be strong enough to associate with Jesus in the public marketplace when he's being driven out and ridiculed? You may be a target, as well, when you associate with him.

However, the great paradox of the Christian faith is that when Jesus becomes to us Lord of all, and we allow him to do with us what he wills, we come alive, and we begin to live. No ridicule from the crowd or discouraging words from others will stop our following because we not only know about Jesus; we know Jesus' love for us personally.

The two blind men were persistent and would not be silenced or deterred. Are you open to pursuing Jesus and following him because he has the words to life? Will you trust him in all areas of your life and be his disciple, or will you try to use him to open doors for your own success and personal gain?

PRAY

Jesus, yes; I want the good stuff in life, and sometimes I want it selfishly. I'm smart enough to know that possessions aren't what make up life or make life worth living. I'll continue to follow, but from a distance, and see what else you may ask me and ask of me. The negativity of the crowds doesn't bother me. If you are who you claim to be, I'll follow. Amen.

CONTEMPLATE

"I do not pray for success; I ask for faithfulness."

St. Teresa of Calcutta

WONDER

1. Have you ever imagined what you would do if you had three wishes? How has your answer to having three wishes changed over the years?
2. How sensitive are you to the "crowds" and opinions of others? Have you ever let the "crowds" affect your decisions?
3. Early on, Sts. James and John and their mother misunderstood what Jesus was talking about in regard to the "kingdom." Have you had misunderstandings about Jesus that have changed over time? What were those?
4. What do you want Jesus to do for you?

8

BUT WHEN THE SON OF MAN COMES, WILL HE FIND FAITH ON EARTH?

Luke 18:8

My wife thinks it's downright strange—crazy, in fact—that I have an odd affection for the run-down motel, the lone one off the interstate, off the exit no one takes, with the faded yellow facade and flickering forty-watt light bulb illuminating little, while seemingly gasping for its last breath of a slow, incandescent death. But for these brief, overnight stays, I don't require much.

When I travel alone to visit family in Texas, it seems my experience is similar at each old-timey motel I stop at. Behind the check-in counter I find the seemingly tired although friendly-enough-to-smile-but-cautious-enough-to-avoid-eye-contact, middle-aged hostess who seems to be a little annoyed that I have actually chosen this motel to spend the evening. In the room immediately behind her where she reclines in between customers entering the establishment I catch a glimpse of the TV and hear the soundtrack of a gameshow that my presence has interrupted. She responds to my request of, "One person, one room, one night, please," with, "Any pets?" I usually think of something clever to say but end up choosing, "No ma'am, just me," to save her the mental anguish of having to respond to my banter. The metal key she hands me dangles from a chain with a large, diamond-shaped, plastic marker on the end, making it clear to anyone within fifty yards that I'm in room number 9, but it's a nice switch from the plastic credit card key found at modern hotels. (I still haven't mastered the art of swiping that card the right way and having the dexterity to spot the green light and turn the knob open before the half-second of opportunity closes.)

The placard under the nondescript motel sign highlighting "Color TV" catches my attention as I drive into the spot reserved for paying customers. The bright yellow door needs a coat of paint, but at least there are no obvious signs of attempted forced entries. My first impression of the room does not meet my already low expectations. I notice the paintings bolted to the wall, neither inspiring confidence nor offering a homey feel to the place. As I step into the room, I cast my gaze toward the bed and notice the painting that hangs above it is right at home in the motel room (and definitely not hanging in any one of those fancy galleries). I cautiously check the bathroom to make sure I'm alone and no one's lurking behind the shower curtain like the Norman Bates character in Hitchcock's *Psycho*. After having spent twelve to fifteen hours in the car with nothing but a stop or two for gas, I decide to stretch my legs and walk to the lone gas station a block away, looking over my shoulder now and again as if any life form would suddenly jump out and attack me. I grab an extra-large package of M&M's and a quart of milk and return to my room to relax with the soft glow of color TV along with the two flies and one moth that will join me for the evening.

I share my experience because it does exhibit faith at some level. Faith, in the first place, that I won't get killed when alone in an unfamiliar place; faith that the room key will work; faith that the motel does indeed have color TV; faith that the place is clean enough that I won't catch some rare tropical disease or plague; and so on.

The word "faith" has come to mean many things to different people. So when speaking of faith, it might be best to take a look at the various meanings or how the word is used so there is no confusion about *religious* faith. I freely admit that I have faith in hundreds of things and countless people, most of whom I don't know personally and likely don't have any direct connection to God. Each morning, for instance, during my twenty-three-minute drive to work, I encounter four traffic signals. Every time I drive through a green light, I actively exhibit faith that the people traveling the crossroads will stop at their red lights. When I enter my place of employment and move the light switch to the up position, I have faith that the light will illuminate, and when I hit the "brew" button on the coffee maker, I do admit that I pray a little that it will start to brew. I don't have to understand electricity for the light to work, nor do I need to have a detailed profile of drivers on the road to know whether or not they're going to obey the laws of driving. It's an act of simple faith.

The faith that is involved in practicing Catholicism is a bit different than the acts of faith described above. Religious faith is both an intellectual assent to theological truths, truths revealed by and about God, and putting those beliefs into action.

Sometimes it's easier to witness faith in action than to intellectually dissect it. The "father of faith" in the Bible is Abraham. He was known as Abram before God changed his name. In Genesis 15:5, God comes to Abram in a vision, takes him outside and says, "Look up at the sky and count the stars, if you can. Just so, he added, will your descendants be." Abram listens to the Word of the Lord and trusts that this will be done. He immediately gathers what is needed for a sacrifice, a covenant meal with God. Soon afterward, in Genesis 15:12, we read, "As the sun was about to set . . ." This is important because we realize that Abram looked up at the stars during the *daytime* when no stars were visible, and he trusted God. If this had occurred at night, Abram would have had some visual evidence of the promise of God. Abram trusted God; he exhibited faith when he saw no physical evidence, and only later would he see God's promise begin to be fulfilled in his lifetime.

An example of faith in the life of an ordinary person whom we encounter in the gospels is a man named Levi. He was a Jewish tax collector, which meant that he collaborated with the Romans, who contracted out the collecting of taxes to private tax collectors. In most cases, the tax collector paid the taxes up front and collected them from the people later. To make this a personally profitable endeavor, tax collectors were notorious for charging more than the actual tax rate. This drew obvious contempt from their fellow countrymen.

In the gospel, Jesus sees Levi sitting at his tax collector's post and summons him with the simple and direct call, "Follow me." Levi's response is recorded in Luke 5:28: "And leaving everything behind, he got up and followed him."

I could argue that Levi's decision to follow Jesus showed even more faith than that of the original four men whom Jesus called on the seashore. Peter, Andrew, James, and John left their nets and boats to follow Jesus, but they did not burn the nets or smash the boats. If this rabbi, Jesus, didn't turn out to be who they thought he might be, they could return to their trade on the sea. Levi, on the other hand, had no alternate plan. The minute he left his post, there was no possibility that any of his countrymen would ever hire him because of his role as collaborator. No Roman would ever employ him, either, for he had left his post.

Levi's response is one without words but not without witness. He hears the call of Jesus to follow, and he responds in a dramatic and an uncompromising way. He shows total trust in the person of Jesus.

Another example of faith can be found in Jesus' life: he was obedient to following the will of God. We might hear that we need to have faith in Jesus, but we can also exhibit the faith *of* Jesus. Jesus' faith in the will of God was total and complete, even when it involved suffering, agony, and the Cross.

In my own life, I can't recall many times when I doubted God's existence, but there were plenty of times when I questioned his timing. It seems that God does not make a habit of informing me about what lies in store for me, my wife, and our family but rather calls me to trust that he knows what he's doing. In looking back in the thirty-plus years since I intentionally gave the reigns over to God, it's crystal clear that he knows what he's doing, which increases my total dependence on him—and I can usually do it with a smile. He has proven himself trustworthy.

But When the Son of Man Comes, Will He Find Faith on Earth?

How about you? Are you ready to make the move to an intellectual assent that Jesus is trustworthy? Are you ready to open your heart to Jesus and put faith into action? You can sit on the fence for only so long. Eventually, not making a decision is your decision.

PRAY

Jesus, I have faith in many things, and in people as well, but am just beginning to learn that I need to be open and trust you. I've heard the stories and witnessed a few examples of faith in action. Show me what I need to do next. Amen.

CONTEMPLATE

"God reveals himself within and through time and is present in the unfolding of events. Faith requires patience and a willingness to wait. Only through time are we able to see how God is at work in each and every person and in each and every situation."

Pope Francis

WONDER

1. In what ways do you exhibit faith in things and people?
2. When has someone lost your trust? What did they do? Was it difficult to trust again?
3. Even the devil believes in Jesus; he chooses not to obey. What's the connection between faith and obedience?
4. Are you ready to trust God and put him first in your life?

9

IF EVEN THE SMALLEST THINGS ARE BEYOND YOUR CONTROL, WHY ARE YOU ANXIOUS ABOUT THE REST?

Luke 12:26

Ah, the illusion of control! We may tend to think we have it all under control, but the truth is, we control very little in this life. If we were to take a step back and gaze toward the heavens, we would immediately realize that there is more than meets the eye. There is much more beyond our scope of comprehension than we'd care to admit. It makes the inner workings and complexities of our homes or workplaces pale in comparison.

By engaging in a life of faith in Jesus, we are called to let go. Our grip on controlling life can be intense. Letting go is an act of faith. But Christians just don't give up on life; we let go and give it to Jesus as we develop trust in him. I admit, it sounds strange, but when we do so, there is a freedom and peace that, as St. Paul says, "surpasses all understanding."

In contrast to the writers of the three synoptic gospels (Matthew, Mark, and Luke), St. John never uses the noun for "faith or belief" in his gospel but rather the verbs "trust and believe." For St. John, believing is an action that one *does*, not an object or thing that one possesses. So often we

hear the phrase or are encouraged to *have faith*, as if we can
pick it up along with a dozen eggs at the store. For St. John,
the translation of the word as *"believing"* is more accurate
than *"having faith."* Believing involves *relationship*, so another
way of thinking about faith is trusting or *entrusting* oneself
to Jesus for everything we need in life. This doesn't happen
all at once: it's a choice we make each day throughout our
lives, although it's important to verbalize it.

The companions of anxiousness are worry, unease, appre-
hension, and frustration. Anxiousness stems from a lack of
trust and leads to disorder and a lack of peace. There are
people and events that concern us because we love them and
care for them, so we are not called to be irresponsible but to
entrust everything to God and live our lives as responsibly
as we can.

One of the benefits of living in New Jersey is that the Garden State has a shore with miles upon miles of boardwalks
and beaches. (One can argue that there are not many benefits
of living in New Jersey, but we take what we can get!) I enjoy
the shore and have good memories as a kid going down there
with my family. I now share those experiences with my wife
and children. Whether it's the shore in New Jersey, Florida,
or California, I have observed four types of people on the
beach. No matter the state, they always seem to be present.

The first person is usually an older gentleman who sits
on a lawn chair near the boardwalk, far away from the water.
Covering his head is a wide brimmed hat. He wears a but-
ton-down plaid shirt with four or five buttons opened, gray
chest hairs popping out through the opening. He has a thick
gold chain or two around his neck, and while he's wearing
a bathing suit, he also sports sandals with black, calf-high

socks. There is activity in the water where the waves crash against the shore, but he is content to sit and read. And then he goes home.

The second type of person I usually see at the beach is a mother surrounded by what seems to be about fifteen small children under the age of seven plus an infant or two in her arms. She's well-equipped with snacks, wipes, juice boxes, and a slew of other necessities that I would never think to bring. While she holds it all together, it appears that every hour on the hour, this mom rises from the oversized blanket and makes her way slowly to the water. As the remnant of a crashing wave reaches her feet, she shuffles back a few inches, giggling as the coolness of the water glides over her toes. She stretches her arms side to side and then, with legs in the locked position, reaches down to put her hands in the water and bring them up to spritz the cool water on her face. She stares off at the horizon for thirty seconds or so and then turns, heading back to the blanket, the kids, the snacks, and what have you.

The next type of people I frequently see make up a happy, adorable, college-age couple with matching blankets and earbuds fixed firmly in their ears. Their loving gazes go from each other's eyes to their phones and back again. Her hair is perfect, and he is fit and trim, while two caffeinated lattes of some foreign coffee concoction are pressed into the sand, which functions nicely as cup holders. This happy couple also rises periodically and, hand in hand, approaches the water. They enter the waves with confidence and lovingly giggle as the water splashes on their mid-sections and over their shorts. They wade out no further than their waists and, still holding hands, rise up a little when the wave lifts them off the sandy security of the ocean floor for two seconds of fun. Quickly they turn their backs to the horizon and head to the safety and security of their blankets, lattes, earbuds, and phones.

The last type of person I find at the beach can be seen hitting the sand running the moment the beach blanket hits the ground and the sneakers and shirt come flying off. Bypassing the older man near the boardwalk, the mom and her gaggle of kids, and the happy couple, he runs directly into the crashing waves and dives into the next one right before it crashes to the ocean floor. The adrenaline pumps wildly through his veins, and the uninhibited excitement of being out in the white water shines in his eyes as he soaks up everything that the waves and water have in store. The joy and ecstasy of being out in there is evident to all.

There is a cost, however, to this person's behavior. Undoubtedly, his hair will get wet, he will most likely end up with some sand in his shorts, and there is a good chance he may get knocked down by a wave or two during the course of his adventure. In comparison to the excitement of the waves and water, these little annoyances are but a minor concern because he comes alive in ways that he could never experience on the security of the beach.

If Even the Smallest Things Are beyond Your Control, Why Are You Anxious about the Rest?

In regard to the spiritual life, I see those same four types of people as they relate to God and faith. Some, like the old man near the boardwalk, don't put forth an effort to investigate what a life of faith is all about or the possibility that God

may be out there. Others, like the mom, just get their feet
wet. They don't want to be perceived as "too religious," and
their contact with God happens during the church services
they attend on Christmas and Easter, if they can make them,
of course. When someone is dying, they'll say a prayer or
send "positive thoughts," but when the crisis subsides, God
is put back in the box until the next calamity comes along.
The happy couple that wades in the water is similar to the
mom except they are more regular with church activities and
confuse membership in a church with an active life of faith in
relationship with Jesus Christ. They have their regular pews,
and we're happy they are present, but Jesus didn't come to
make us churchgoers. He calls us to follow him no matter
where our yes to him takes us, even if it's to unchartered
waters, away from the security of our comfort zones.

In many regards, people like the fourth person are who
we are talking about when it comes to being followers of
Jesus. When we follow Jesus, when we read his Word, stay
connected through the sacraments, pray with fervor, and
surround ourselves with others active in this journey of faith,
we are captured and compelled to follow him because he has
the words of eternal life. He is the resurrection and the life,
and in following him, we find what previous followers have
discovered: a joy and purpose in life that surpasses all understanding. We may get knocked down, criticized, persecuted,
or shut out of social groups, but we gladly accept it, for we
not only know about God but we know him intimately and
follow him wherever he leads.

Life is full of complexity and uncertainty, and Jesus asks
us to trust in him for everything. In your discernment of
who Jesus is and what he asks, will you trust in him? Or

will you trust in yourself, your good looks, your money, or your connections in order to just get through life? Will you continue sitting on the fence?

The question, of course, is not where you are now but in what direction you are heading. What's preventing you from getting your feet wet, wading in, or choosing to go all-in for Jesus?

"If even the smallest things are beyond your control, why are you anxious about the rest?" (Lk 12:26).

PRAY

Jesus, if I'm going to follow you, I want to do it right. Doing anything in half measures is a waste of time. I'm willing to take the next steps, get my feet wet, and go further. Help me along the way. Amen.

CONTEMPLATE

"All of my life, I've seen possibilities where others choose not to. Growing up extremely poor with a single mom working tirelessly to provide for six kids, I knew that my circumstances were meant to teach me something. To fuel me, not hinder me. I wasn't always a good student, however, education comes in many forms, if you choose to recognize the lesson. For instance, I've learned to base my decisions on whether or not I'm passionate about the outcome. People tell me that I have an intensity or tenacity about me—and it's true. The minute I decide to take action, in my mind the story is already written. I just have to physically get there, no matter what. I am a living, breathing example of what happens when you choose to see obstacles as opportunities and let your faith in God and your faith in yourself align."

Bill Hynes, CEO of Think Loud Development LLC and US Veteran

WONDER

1. Where are you "on the beach" right now in your life with regard to faith in Jesus?
2. What's the difference between "having faith" and "entrusting yourself to Jesus"?
3. Why is it difficult to let go of old ways of doing things?
4. Are you ready to trust Jesus with your life?

10

BUT WHO DO YOU SAY THAT I AM?

Matthew 16:15

Jesus does not just want to be friends. Jesus does not need fans. He does not desire seat-fillers at Mass. Jesus doesn't need us to wear jewelry with his image on it. He doesn't need the dollar some throw in the basket at church. Jesus doesn't need people to admire his moral teaching nor to post his image incessantly on social media. Jesus doesn't need us to sing songs about him, complete with hand motions. He doesn't need people who "love" *him* but dislike his Church. Jesus doesn't need people who pick and choose what they like about his teaching but disregard the rest.

Who is this Jesus who demands total commitment?

I believe he is God.

I believe in his Immaculate Conception, and I believe in his Resurrection. I believe.

I believe in the Catholic Church, the community of believers who have borne witness through the centuries to his life, death, and resurrection, those who wrote the gospels and the rest of the New Testament, those who continue to witness to his presence.

"But who do you say that I am?"

C. S. Lewis, an Oxford medieval literature scholar, writer, and former atheist of the last century, expanded on a "trilemma" that was around for one hundred years before him. This trilemma focuses on who the person of Jesus was by presenting three options: Jesus is a liar, a lunatic, or Lord.

How often do we hear it propositioned that Jesus was a good man, a fine moral teacher, but certainly not God? Not to go through Lewis's argument word for word, but simply stated, if Jesus is not God, then it would be silly to categorize him as a good teacher, for he claimed to be God, and if he is not God, that makes him a liar. Jesus forgave people's offenses against God, which God alone can forgive; if he is not God that makes him a liar. Jesus promised those who follow him eternal life. If he is not God, than he is a liar and perhaps closer to Lucifer, promising others life everlasting, which he can't deliver. Good moral teachers are not known for their deception.

Perhaps Jesus was a lunatic or at least one who was deluded about who he was. We all know crazy people. We may not know they're crazy at first, or self-deluded, but it comes to the forefront pretty quickly. Was Jesus deluded? Was he crazy? Sincere, but crazy nonetheless? Well, when we look at his words and actions, we discover profound insight into the human condition: compassion for the sick and marginalized, love for God, and love for neighbor. He shows and speaks about justice for the oppressed, forgiveness to the sinner, and harsh words for hypocrites despite their plotting and persecution of him. Jesus is called honest and forthright only once, and this is by those who were against him.

A rational look at cultures and societies in which Christianity has taken root reveals a profound respect for the dignity of the human person. Within such cultures, the rights and roles of women are elevated, religious freedom is encouraged and protected, and forgiveness, justice, and mercy are sought. These are the hallmarks of a Christian culture. Are these societies perfect? Of course not, because perfection comes only in heaven, but as G. K. Chesterton so beautifully said, "The Christian ideal has not been tried and found wanting. It has been found difficult; and left untried."[5]

And then there is the empty tomb.

For those who have accepted Christ as Lord and God through faith, there is the confidence and evidence of God's presence in their lives. For many, that is enough. But even in the Apostles Creed, one of the earliest declarations of what we believe about Jesus, we read, ". . . born of the Virgin Mary, suffered under Pontius Pilate, was crucified, died and was buried; he descended into hell; on the third day he rose again. . . ." Not a word about the teaching of Jesus nor his miracles or parables. The empty tomb is key.

While I wasn't present at the tomb, I know that something happened based on how those early followers acted afterward. All of the apostles, save St. John, gave their lives in martyrdom for Jesus, whom they witnessed suffering, dying, and resurrected from the dead. There is something there that is real. The witness of the saints and martyrs down through the ages reveals a truth that points to the power of the resurrection.

But Who Do You Say That I Am?

The early disciples of Jesus encountered the risen Lord, and they were forever changed. It's not about a particular day or hour in which we acknowledge Jesus as Lord, for throughout the gospels, we see even demons acknowledging Jesus as Lord. Lip service is not enough. Stating the truth that Jesus is Lord is accurate, but if even the demons acknowledge him as such, what's the difference? Disciples of Jesus in every generation are known by their love for one another, a love initiated and completed in Jesus Christ. The words of our lips need to be followed by the actions of our lives.

I knew about Jesus for many years. Where I was mentally and emotionally as a young person in grade school and in the early part of high school was pretty normal, but it became apparent in the latter part of high school that something was missing that sports, grades, and other activities couldn't fill.

In faith, I took the next step and said in my heart of hearts, *Lord, if you are real and alive today, let me know.* Over the next few months, people came into my life here and there who were normal, well-educated, had well-paying jobs, and spoke about Jesus in a personal way. I knew that I wanted that, too. I started to do the things that these active Catholics did, like have a consistent prayer time, read a chapter of the gospel each day, memorize scripture verses, attend Mass daily, and go to Confession regularly. I was making a daily choice to love God.

I can tell you it was the best decision I've ever made, for it has informed every decision I've made since. You, too, can make that decision and begin a journey anew.

PRAY

Jesus, I'll take these next steps and follow you. I'll commit to doing the things that will help me know you better. Be with me along the way. Amen.

CONTEMPLATE

"Christianity, unlike any other religion in the world, begins with catastrophe and defeat. Sunshine religions and psychological inspirations collapse in calamity and wither in adversity. But the Life of the Founder of Christianity, having begun with the Cross, ends with the empty tomb and victory."

Venerable Fulton J. Sheen

WONDER

1. Who do you say that Jesus is?
2. What are the ramifications in the short term for choosing a life with him?
3. What are the questions and challenges you have to face because of this decision?
4. Who is going to support you and help keep you accountable in your life of faith?

THREE

Complete Control

11

WHY DO YOU CALL ME, "LORD, LORD," BUT NOT DO WHAT I COMMAND?

Luke 6:46

Any athlete can attest that the hardest, most demanding coaches draw the most out of them in preparation for competition. I've been told that those who take ballet or are involved in music at a high level feel the same way about their instructors and mentors. Most athletes come to the playing field with tools similar to those of their competitors: excellent physical condition, knowledge of the game and its nuances, and a desire to win. What separates the good from the great? The cook from the master chef? The average dancer from the *prima ballerina assoluta*? The general orchestra member from the concertmaster? If the tools and knowledge are basically the same, it usually comes down to the mindset: the pursuit of excellence and, in some fields, the will to win.

In following Christ, it's holiness, the desire to be a saint and to be so filled with the presence of God, the Holy Spirit, that when one observes your life, what they see is not you but Christ who lives in you.

Acknowledging that Jesus is Lord and choosing to follow him is the beginning of a new phase in our lives and the start of our discipleship. St. Paul writes, "Do not conform yourselves to this age but be transformed by the renewal of your mind, that you may discern what is the will of God, what is good and pleasing and perfect" (Rom 12:2). This new life is certainly a cause for joy, yet the journey to develop the *mind of Christ* is one that has challenges both in the way we live our lives and how we see the world and circumstances. This interior journey to be *"Christlike"* and *"holy"* is difficult, but we are not called to do it alone. The Holy Spirit makes his home in our hearts and desires to transform us into who we are meant to be in Christ along with the community of believers.

Throughout the four gospels, Jesus is welcoming to the multitudes, consoling to the weak and ignorant, merciful when he sees the hungry crowds, and forgiving when he's with marginalized people one-on-one. When it comes to his inner circle, the disciples and, in particular, the apostles, Jesus is demanding.

The plan of Jesus to share God's message of redemption and forgiveness with the world after his death and resurrection will come through these twelve and through others who will follow. The idea that following Christ is easy and undemanding is not to know Jesus or to be unfamiliar with his Word. Fulfilling? Yes. Joyful? Certainly. Easy? No. For following Christ demands a total reevaluation of those attitudes, thoughts, and actions that have been formed in us through the secular world and not formed through God's word and the teaching of his church, developed over the past two thousand years.

Calling Jesus *Lord* is good, true, and proper, for he *is* Lord. However, there is a difference between proclaiming Jesus as

Lord and adjusting our lives to his lordship. We are either Christ-oriented or dis-oriented.

In the gospels, when Jesus is teaching there are various responses from those who encounter him. Some hear his words and see his signs yet refuse to believe. There are those who begin to believe yet don't fully recognize Jesus' identity. A few come to believe but refuse to publicly acknowledge Jesus as Lord, and then there are others who see, believe, and are known as his disciples. The last group Jesus praises are those who believe without ever seeing him in the flesh or witnessing his signs and wonders. These disciples believe on the basis of hearing the words of Jesus and seeing the life witness of those who follow.

Living like Jesus is a process. There is no instant discipleship. As Catholics, we eagerly point to Jesus and to others called saints who have been faithful to living like Christ and witnessed to his love in an exemplary fashion. This was not by their own efforts, of course, but they surrendered their wills to his and the Holy Spirit animated their lives.

In the question Jesus poses, he asks, "Why do you call me, 'Lord, Lord,' and not do what I command?" Jesus gives an example of what "doing what I command" looks like, and it's grueling: "I will show you what someone is like who comes to me, listens to my words, and acts on them. That one is like a person building a house, who dug deeply and laid the foundation on rock; when the flood came, the river burst against that house but could not shake it because it had been well built. But the one who listens and does not act is like a person who built a house on the ground without a foundation. When the river burst against it, it collapsed at once and was completely destroyed" (Lk 6:47–49).

I've done my share of manual labor up to this point in my life, from working in an industrial factory to loading and unloading 18-wheelers in the shipping dock of Ethylene Corporation. I can honestly say that I've never had to dig a foundation.

What I once imagined was required in digging a foundation in the Middle East is far different from what I now know it to be after a few experiences in Israel. Not that I thought Jesus would start up the tractor and use hydraulics to dig through the soil, but I clearly underestimated the labor, sweat, and time it took to prepare a foundation in the hard soil of the Middle East with primitive tools. It's imperative to mention this because Jesus compares *hearing* and *doing*, which sounds reasonably easy, to the labor involved in digging through hard clay down to bedrock to lay the foundation.

These words would have been sobering to those who thought following Jesus would be easy. Foundations are built in the summer in the Middle East to avoid the rain. The weather is suitable, but the ground is not due to its high clay content and bone-dry conditions. The book of Leviticus describes the soil as "*as hard as bronze*" (Lv 26:19, emphasis added). The primitive tools made digging difficult at best, and combined with the intense sun bearing down on the workers' heads, it made the temptation to go just a few feet down rather than all the way to rock appealing. The easy way is almost always appealing. After all, clay is similar to rock. Most homes were simple one-story edifices, so it would have been easy to take a short cut and think that the hard clay would suffice to hold up the walls and roof.

What happens when you don't dig down to bedrock? The winter rain comes, small trickles of water rapidly turn into streams of flowing mud, and soon after, rivers. As the waters rise, they begin to consume the clay below and soften it, thus compromising the foundation . . . and it all comes tumbling down!

The foundation is undetected when life is peaceful and predictable. The storm hits both houses; both are susceptible. Like the houses, we are each exposed to the storms of life. The storms will hit; we just don't know when.

Why Do You Call Me "Lord, Lord," but Not Do What I Command?

The words of Jesus function as a warning to those who trust in themselves. The religious leadership of Jesus' day would have taken his words as a warning against their alliance with foreign rulers rather than trusting in God. The good news is that Jesus' words also provide a way out of the storm, offering a new foundation with the person and words of Jesus Christ.

Reading, studying, and contemplating the words of Jesus help us begin to undergo a transformation and renewal of our minds, of how we see the world. But that is not enough. The followers of Jesus hear and begin to put that word into practice. Obedience to Jesus' word is not a hindrance to joy, but the path to freedom. It gives us the ability to withstand the torrents in life. What areas of your life are not under Jesus' lordship?

PRAY

Lord Jesus, help me to do what you command. Without your spirit, I can't make progress. Send your Holy Spirit to be by my side so I may do all that you command. Amen.

CONTEMPLATE

"A Christian isn't a person who simply follows some commandments, but is a person who tries to act, think, and love like Christ."

Pope Francis

WONDER

1. Who were some of the demanding teachers or coaches you have had in life? How did their influence impact you?
2. To what extent do you see responding to the level of commitment Jesus asks for as *labor*?
3. Why do people assume that religion is an escape from the storms of life?
4. What is Jesus calling you to do that may be challenging?

12

WHY DO YOU NOTICE THE SPLINTER IN YOUR BROTHER'S EYE, BUT DO NOT PERCEIVE THE WOODEN BEAM IN YOUR OWN EYE?

Matthew 7:3

I enjoy the phrase that goes something along the lines of "I was a people person . . . but people ruined that for me." If only life weren't so full of people who are imperfect and annoying! To be honest, I *am* a people person and by nature, I don't get annoyed easily. I think a healthy sense of humor allows me to avoid some of the judgmental attitudes that others may experience. While I may credit my easygoing nature as a reason why I'm not often judgmental of others, for a follower of Jesus, it's not optional.

In living out the call to follow Jesus, which is discipleship, some people view themselves as judge and juror, marking every imperfection and flaw of others. This is true today, and apparently, it was true two thousand years ago, for Jesus speaks some pretty harsh words to those who spend a great deal of time pointing out the faults of others while failing to examine their own failings.

If we are serious about following Jesus, we need to take a critical look at ourselves and consider how uncharitable we can be at times, both verbally and nonverbally. As Christians, we give our entire beings to God: body, mind, and soul. The critical look is not easy, for it may reveal some flaws that we'll need to change with the help of the Holy Spirit. As claimed in the anonymous proverb that "a man who is his own lawyer may have a fool for a client," so, too, we are not always the best candidates to discern where we need to adjust and change.

Many committed Catholics have spiritual directors, often priests, sisters, or trained laypersons who can gently assist and help others grow spiritually. The spiritual director can aid in identifying areas of needed spiritual growth as well as areas of unnecessary guilt. A spiritual director can offer a perspective that is honest and charitable, pointing us to Jesus.

The good news is that we are not called to "fix" ourselves. We are responsible for the depth of our relationships with God, but the key element is to be open to the Holy Spirit, changing and molding us from within. Any "fixing" we may need is God's responsibility. We must be open and sensitive to the movement of the Holy Spirit, who will reveal to us in such ways that we will know it is him calling us to change. Sometimes, his prompts will be subtle, and other times, he will use whatever means necessary to form us into the image of Jesus.

St. John XXIII remarked, "See everything, overlook a great deal, correct a little."[6] This is from the pope who was responsible for the global Church! We need to correct when people are hurting themselves and others. We must not be silent when there is injustice. In fact, if a friend will not tolerate us speaking out against injustice or evil then the price of that friendship is too high to be morally acceptable.

We can't let everything go in the name of tolerance. The wisdom, of course, is in discerning when to correct and, more importantly, *how* we correct. In the Church, it's referred to as fraternal correction, which Jesus also talks about at length later on in Matthew's gospel.

Why Do You Notice the Splinter in Your Brother's Eye, but Do Not Perceive the Wooden Beam in Your Own Eye?

In our first stages of discipleship, we are learning how to develop "the mind of Christ," as St. Paul puts it (1 Cor 2:16). This includes beginning to adjust the ways we see others and ourselves. Jesus doesn't pull out a long laundry list of bad behaviors, but he asks a simple and direct question about our judgmental natures. How can we so easily see the flaws in others yet so easily ignore our own?

As a person who has worked in and for the Church for close to thirty years, I have come across laypeople and clergy alike who truly live out lives of faith, entrusting themselves to divine providence and following God's Word. Where they go, peace follows. Faith is not an empty word but a lived encounter with God, which continues to attract even people with no religious backgrounds. The joy that emanates from their faith in Jesus is evident to all and is not turned off the minute people leave or parishioners exit the building. They lead with love. Their witness, which is bound to Jesus, is enough to convert hearts. No word of judgment is needed, and when words are spoken, they seem to flow from the chambers of the Sacred Heart of Jesus himself.[7]

I also know of a cast of characters who have not undergone that transformation of the Holy Spirit, and a different "fruit" is evident in their lives. Due to their status in the Church, they are under the illusion that they can control everything, including people. Unfortunately, individuals like this often use God as a justification for their own neuroses. They believe that living the faith can be planned out and evaluated with the precision of a grade school science project. Often, they are judgmental of everyone but themselves and use their position to threaten others. Perhaps because of their own wounded pasts, they use fear and intimidation to coerce their agendas, which are cloaked as "God's will." While we need to pray for them and their conversion we need to ask a critical question: Which type of person do you want to be?

One of the major ramifications of original sin is blindness to our own sinfulness. Jesus said, "Do you have eyes and not see, ears and not hear?" (Mk 8:18) and "I came into this world for judgment, so that those who do not see might see" (Jn 9:39). It takes humility to acknowledge that we need to be open to the Holy Spirit transforming us from within and that we need others to help us realize our own defects and flaws. In humility, we need to be open to the constructive criticism of others who love us and even of those who don't. God uses everything and everyone to draw us close to himself. We must recognize those times in our own lives when our own agendas are not in line with God's will. We must listen to others who love us and who draw us away from distorted images of our own perceived perfection.

How did you feel when you were criticized by others who didn't know your whole story? I know I've been guilty of making those judgments toward others. Remember, also, those who let their example of Christian behavior witness to your life.

Pope Francis often cites the examen as part of his nightly routine. This specific prayer is based on Jesuit spirituality.[8] The Jesuits are a religious order founded by St. Ignatius of Loyola more than five hundred years ago and are often called the Society of Jesus. The examen asks the person to do basically five things at the end of each day:

1. Become aware of God's presence.
2. Review the day with gratitude.
3. Pay attention to your emotions.
4. Choose one feature of the day and pray from it.
5. Look toward tomorrow.

The examen is a valuable yet pretty simple routine that helps us to reflect and be mindful of those areas where we have been critical of others, ask forgiveness, and begin anew each day. Saints aren't made overnight.

PRAY

Jesus, be Lord of every aspect of my life and especially those thoughts and attitudes that originate in my mind and can affect my view of others. Give me the wisdom to know when to speak in love and when to be quiet. Amen.

CONTEMPLATE

"What's wrong with the world? I am."

G. K. Chesterton

WONDER

1. Do you get easily annoyed with the behavior of others? If so, what can you do to reduce that?
2. Do you become easily annoyed at your own behavior? How can turning to Christ help you?
3. Why can it be difficult to accept criticism from others with regard to our behavior?
4. How can you remember to keep your own affairs in order before you criticize others?

13

WILL NOT GOD THEN SECURE THE RIGHTS OF HIS CHOSEN ONES WHO CALL OUT TO HIM DAY AND NIGHT?

Luke 18:7

When I was four or five years old, I noticed that my parents were both sitting at the dining room table reading the paper and discussing the news of the day. They were clearly not using the car. I proceeded to the kitchen, grabbed the car keys off a hook, and motioned to my dad that I was heading out on the open road. I gave him the head nod, smiled, turned, and proceeded out the back door, planning to walk down a few steps and onward to our blue 1972 Pontiac station wagon, which was parked in the unpaved driveway.

I'd made it to the second step when my sensation of gravity was suddenly suspended. My dad had caught me by my collar and slowly lifted me straight up in the air. The next thing I knew, my feet landed firmly on the *terra firma* of our dining room floor.

The conversation then began with me questioning the wisdom of my father for not letting me use the car, which neither he nor my mother was using. His reply was a shaking of his head and a firm "No." My rebuttal was tears and loud wailing, which didn't change his decision.

In hindsight, it's clear that he acted out of one motivation: love. He knew the pitfalls associated with a young child trying to drive a car: insurance liabilities, my inability to see over the steering wheel, and the danger I posed to myself and others among a host of other issues. In love, he acted in a way that was best for me, as he would do for the rest of his life. As I grew older, I learned that love is what motivated both him and my mother.

At times, I confess, I still act like a five-year-old child when it comes to making sense of God's will, injustice, and of course, suffering. But I have learned that my ways are not God's ways and that Jesus is all too familiar with God's will, injustice, and of course, suffering. I also know that the love that motivated my dad also motivates God.

When you know you're loved, when you entrust yourself to love, there is waiting. There is a degree of uncertainty. There is also an opportunity to trust. Love is perhaps refined in those hours and days and weeks and even years of patience or long-suffering, as it was called in days gone by.

There are no easy answers to why God allows injustice and suffering. If it were not for the Cross, I don't know how I'd try to make sense of it. Saying something is "God's will" usually does little to comfort the afflicted, especially if they have no relationship with God. Our response to injustice should be to help alleviate suffering and advocate for integrity and fair treatment of others. When there is a crisis in the world, God usually responds by raising up saints, the likes of you and me.

According to some scholars, the most ancient book in the Bible is the book of Job, which addresses the question of suffering. When God speaks out of the whirlwind, he does something unexpected. Instead of comforting Job emotionally, he goes one better. He teaches him truth.

God asks Job roughly seventy-seven questions (depending on sentence structure) as a rhetorical device to teach Job a great truth. The truth is that God is God and Job is not. There are questions concerning ten or twelve animals as well. The strength of the horse, the stubbornness of the donkey, and even the birthplace of mountain goats are but a few of the questions God uses to reveal to Job that if God has intimate knowledge and care for these animals, *how much more* God cares for him.

Will Not God Then Secure the Rights of His Chosen Ones Who Call Out to Him Day and Night?

In the verses preceding the parable of the Persistent Widow, we notice that Luke writes, "He spoke a parable to *them*," indicating that Jesus is addressing his disciples. The vulnerability of widows in ancient times is well-noted as is the requirement of God's people to uphold their rights. In the parable, the judge neither fears God nor has any regard for man. He only cares for himself. We can easily imagine that this widow has need of some sort of legal protection; perhaps someone is threatening to take her land in payment of a debt. She must deal with a judge who is by nature unlikely to be interested in the problems of a marginalized and socially insignificant widow.

As with many of Jesus' parables, we hear the internal dialogue of the judge who says to himself, "While it is true that I neither fear God nor respect any human being, because this widow keeps bothering me I shall deliver a just decision for her lest she finally come and strike me" (Lk 18:4–5). The judge may be referring metaphorically to the damage the widow will do to his reputation. The Semitic expression "to blacken someone's face" means to bring shame on someone. The widow's *continual* coming would be making him look bad—and in the Middle Eastern culture, shame is to be avoided at all costs and is the ultimate "black eye."

If Jesus is recasting language familiar to the religious leaders, he is asking a question that demands a negative answer: "Will God be patient? No!" Since the great hope of the Christian is that we will not receive justice but mercy, why does Jesus portray the people of God as crying out for justice? It may seem inappropriate for Christians to be hoping for this, but it is important for Christians to understand that God values justice as well as mercy. He reminds us that, ultimately, God will deal with the wrongs that have been done. Those who will not come to God for mercy will receive his justice. If this *unjust* judge even said yes, then what shall we expect our loving God to say?

Fundamentally, prayer is a way of living out and persevering in our faith. The call of all believers is to persevere in that belief. In the story of Job and the parable, Jesus has reminded us that God is merciful, just, and loyal to his people. Our faith requires us to trust God while living in an unjust world. St. Catherine of Siena reminds us that "Everything comes from love, all is ordained for the salvation of man, God does nothing without this goal in mind."[9] Thank God that we were treated with patience while we were living in unbelief.

PRAY

Lord Jesus, I'll leave sorting out the injustice of this world to your care. Help me to trust even when I don't understand, for I know you are familiar with suffering and injustice. Remind me often to be a person of justice, and open my eyes to those people whom I can assist and advocate for during my time on earth. Amen.

CONTEMPLATE

"Do not be provoked by evildoers; do not envy those who do wrong. Like grass they wither quickly; like green plants they wilt away. Trust in the Lord and do good that you may dwell in the land and live secure. Find your delight in the Lord who will give you your heart's desire. Commit your way to the Lord; trust in him and he will act and make your righteousness shine like the dawn, your justice like noonday. Be still before the Lord; wait for him."

Psalm 37:1–7

WONDER

1. Have questions of suffering and injustice ever proved a roadblock to your belief in a just God?
2. Considering the Cross, is it fair to ask "Why me?" when we suffer? Why?
3. Why did God provide Job with truth instead of an emotional experience?
4. Can faith exist without doubt?

14

WHY DO YOU HARBOR EVIL THOUGHTS?

Matthew 9:4

On most Thursdays for the past ten years or so, early in the morning, before the commuter traffic becomes unbearable and preceding the glimmer of the first rays of the sun peering over the Watchung Mountains, you'll find me in the city of Plainfield, New Jersey, once known as the "Queen City." The drive from my home to Plainfield is only about twenty minutes, yet because of the turmoil that took place there in the late 1960s and the poverty and gangs that exist there today, the surrounding area becomes more derelict as one descends from suburbia into the city, with its abandoned storefronts and pockmarked streets. Day laborers stand on a number of corners and barren parking lots hoping to be chosen for work, enduring the summer's brutal humidity and heat as well as the winter's sub-zero temperatures as they cast eyes on any and all who drive by.

What brings me to the Queen City is a convent on the corner of Sixth Street and Liberty. Relinquished by Irish Sisters who laid the foundation in brick and mortar a century earlier and who settled here to minister to the Irish and German immigrants, it is an active convent forming the contemplative branch of the Missionary of Charity Sisters founded by St. Teresa of Calcutta. For more than twenty-five years, women from all walks of life, backgrounds, education, and cultures have responded to a call to grow in holiness as "Contemplative" Missionaries of Charity in this convent, a house of formation.[10] These contemplative sisters lead a life of prayer, silence, solitude, fasting, and penance. While they are actively engaged in the community, the majority of their life is spent in prayer, uniting in heart and mind and spirit with Jesus, their spouse in Eucharistic Adoration.

In this convent, I have had the privilege of teaching sisters from Africa, the Philippines, Mexico, the Czech Republic, Spain, South Korea, Argentina, France, Bosnia, Ireland, the United States, and Poland. Here, among these joyful, loving women who are responding to a call, a religious vocation, war is waged and battles are fought.

It's easy to be fooled by these women in formation, with their white saris that look like St. Teresa's religious habit, only without the traditional three blue stripes adorning the borders. They always open the door with smiling faces, and as I approach the table where I sit to teach, I am greeted by a warm cup of coffee, a glass of water, and a small sandwich bag of assorted cookies for my children. Their warm welcome, joyful expressions, and eagerness to learn can easily fool the outsider as to the tenacity and firmness of resolve that these women possess to be holy and to love Jesus with their whole beings.

It's humbling to be in their presence each week as I open to a chapter in the Bible, draw out meaning from the text, and in some small way assist them in discovering an insight, some spiritual nugget that may be helpful in their formation.

As I walk in, I always notice the warm note welcoming me by name on the small chalk board that is affixed to the wall directly under the crucifix. The words "I Thirst" written below the crossbeam of the crucifix reminds me of Jesus' and this Society's "thirst" for souls. The joy, prayer, and laughter we share are evidence to God's presence. There are no electronics in the convent, no cell phones or computers, and—to the amazement of my children and students whom I've brought there for Eucharistic Adoration and evening prayer—no mirrors.

Why Do You Harbor Evil Thoughts?

If you don't realize that you're in a battle, you've already lost. The serious life of sacrifice and prayer that these women undertake is to allow their heart's souls, strength, and minds to be united to Jesus. If you think it's easy to develop the mind of Jesus, then you've never tried. The outward appearance of these sisters in formation, and of the professed sisters whose religious habit is the same as worn by St. Teresa of Calcutta herself, is not in and of itself a magical cloak of holiness. While each article of clothing does point to something deeper and has its own significance, it is a reminder of the spiritual battle that they wage. I personally know of no group of people who are as committed to following Jesus and abandoning all to him as these women. When they speak of the interior spiritual life, I listen. When I observe them pray, I'm preached to. When I witness their smiles, I'm edified. When I see their sacrifices and poverty, I'm humbled. When I hear them sing, I glimpse heaven.

The battle we fight is an interior battle with our own egos, spiritual forces, and evil. It's not politically correct to mention "demonic forces" or "evil spirits" in today's world, but they are a reality. Jesus mentions them with regularity, as does St. Paul, so maybe the skeptic should look again.

This battle of aligning our wills to that of Jesus is difficult. It takes prayer, discipline, and the Holy Spirit to continue the battle when "feelings" of God's love and presence have long ceased. Bl. Miriam Teresa Demjanovich, a recently beatified sister from New Jersey, wrote, "No will, no thought, no desire, save his!"[11] The interior life of a follower of Jesus is a constant struggle between our wills and the will of God. Many initial followers fade away when they are faced with the interior life to which Christ, through grace, calls us.

St. Paul documents his own struggle quite clearly in his letter to the Romans. In chapter 7, he uses the personal pronoun "I" twenty-eight times in verses 7–25. "For I do not do the good I want, but the evil I do not want is what I do" (Rom 7:19). St. Paul was fervent and ardent in his efforts to do the right thing but found himself coming up short. Thanks be to God that his letter to the Romans didn't end with chapter 7, for in chapter 8, he reveals what is the "key," what he discovered when the proverbial light bulb went on for him.

In Romans chapter 8, St. Paul references the Holy Spirit close to a dozen times. "If the Spirit of the one who raised Jesus from the dead dwells in you, the one who raised Christ from the dead will give life to your mortal bodies also, through his Spirit that dwells in you" (Rom 8:11). The "key" for St. Paul was that he was not designed to "go it alone" apart from the grace of God. St. Paul was sincere in his desire to be holy, but he was trying to accomplish this apart from God's help, if you will. What St. Paul came to realize is that he just needed to do one thing and that was be open to the Holy Spirit and allow God to work in and through him. We are called to do the same.

No one has ever perfectly aligned human will completely to God's will except Mary, the Mother of Jesus. While perfection in this life may not be expected, the desire and will to be holy is necessary. We must begin to humbly discipline ourselves to a position to be formed by God and his church, through prayer and obedience.

Jesus calls us to this battle, and he provides the grace through the sacraments in order that we be conformed to his image and likeness. When we advance in this struggle and die to our egos and "wills," something odd happens: we begin to come alive.

Are you humble enough to seek God's assistance in striving to be Christlike, to be holy? Will you harbor evil thoughts against others? Will you fight the good fight to which Christ calls us?

PRAY

Jesus, it is evident that what you ask of me is difficult, but you've equipped me by sending me the Holy Spirit. The more I try to get rid of bad or evil thoughts, the more they seem to appear, so I know I can't do this alone. Send me help; I'm open and willing to take these steps toward becoming like you. Amen.

CONTEMPLATE

"The reason we have not yet become saints is because we have not understood what it is to love. We think we do, but we do not. To love is to conform oneself to the beloved in the most intimate manner of which we are capable; to have no views but his views; no thoughts but his thoughts, no desires but his desires, no likes but his likes; no wants but his wants; no hopes but his hopes; no will but his will."

Bl. Miriam Teresa

WONDER

1. Do you find it difficult to control your thoughts? In what way?
2. How do you deal with other people's negative thoughts and even with your own?
3. What do you think of the idea that this struggle may be a sign that you're making progress in the spiritual life? Does that thought bring you comfort?
4. How can you allow yourself to be more open to God and obedient to his word?

15
WHY DID YOU DOUBT?

Matthew 14:31

Throughout the Old Testament, there are multiple "biblical call narratives." God chose men and women throughout salvation history to deliver his message, and as we read three or four of these biblical calls, we begin to identify a pattern. God calls a person, who usually has no previous preparation, and he calls them when they least expect it. God's word is spoken to an individual either directly by God or through a messenger, and then they are commissioned for the task God called them to carry out. In almost every case, there is an objection, for the person feels ill-equipped for the task. From a human point of view, these people *are* ill-equipped, and they say something along the lines of, "But Lord, I am too young," or too old, or can't speak, and the list of objections goes on. God reassures them and seals his reassurance with his word.

If you examine the calls of Abraham, Moses, Gideon, Jeremiah, Isaiah, and Jonah, you'll identify the pattern. Why isn't a burning bush enough? Why isn't a visitation from an angel enough? I guess it speaks to the fact that we all need reassurance because we can all doubt, and God is well aware of this.

Our encounter with Jesus causes us to make some changes in our lives, and this affects others as well. We hope others are supportive of our decision to follow Jesus, but that's not always the case. At times during our journey of faith, we may feel isolated, alone, and even abandoned, which is tough to deal with and may cause us to question if we've chosen the right path.

While it's not always the case, we can have an emotional experience with God, which by its very nature is moving and powerful. However, when a crisis occurs in our lives, we tend not to fall back on a retreat experience or an *emotional high* when we "felt close to God" to get through the difficulty or moments of doubt. In these moments of doubt, we must remind ourselves and rely on what we know to be true. We must also rely on a community of believers who are also convinced of the truth of the Gospel and have been through moments of doubt and feelings of abandonment.

Moments of doubt will come to us all, as they came to the likes of St. Thomas, who has been known as "doubting Thomas" for the past two thousand years after initially doubting the Resurrection. He is still referred to as "doubting Thomas" even though he was martyred for his faith in Jesus after a long life of missionary service that brought him to India in the late first century.

In the writings of St. Teresa of Calcutta, we find that she had no words to express the depths of the *darkness* she encountered through much of her life, which only increases our admiration for her joyful service, a true mark of authentic faith. This darkness can be expressed as a lack of *feeling* the presence of God. St. Teresa stands firmly in the tradition of St. John of the Cross, a Spanish priest and mystic of the sixteenth century, who labeled his feelings of abandonment by God a *"dark night of the soul."*[12] Saints and mystics go through periods when they don't *feel* God's presence for an extended time, so we shouldn't be surprised if we experience such dryness as well.

Why Did You Doubt?

Jesus poses the question, "Why did you doubt?" to St. Peter, the future head of the Church and the man whose name literally means rock! It appears plain to see that Peter, the rock, was sinking into the sea after walking on it for a time at Jesus' command. The text reveals that, "But when he saw how strong the wind was he became frightened; and, beginning to sink, he cried out, 'Lord, save me!'" (Mt 14:30).

Perhaps the lesson for us is to keep our eyes fixed on Jesus in the midst of whatever storms come our way. Hopefully, through the experience of moments of doubt, we will realize that we are not alone and we can come out stronger on the other side. We will be better equipped to assist others who may have doubts as well. St. Paul urges the young disciple Timothy to "compete well for the faith. Lay hold of eternal life, to which you were called when you made the noble confession in the presence of many witnesses" (1 Tm 6:12).

Jesus himself is praying for us not lose hope! "I pray not only for them, but also for those who will believe in me through their word, so that they may all be one, as you, Father, are in me and I in you, that they also may be in us, that the world may believe that you sent me" (Jn 17:20–21).

If you look for the word "doubt" in the New Testament, you will see that the term has been used to translate four different Greek words, which are themselves quite distinct from one another. Not one of these describes a situation where a person has taken a deliberate stand against faithfulness. The word is used in connection with an individual who is puzzled and trying to make sense out of a confusing event. The word carries the connotation of uncertainty rather than the outright rejection of Jesus or his message. Sometimes the word carries the meaning of bewilderment or confusion. In Matthew 14:31, when Jesus asks the question "Why did you doubt?" the word used for doubt in the original Greek is *distazo*, which is used only twice in the New Testament. This has frequently been read as a rebuke of Peter's lack of faith, but understood correctly in the historical context, the idea of hesitation or uncertainty is being conveyed. Jesus is communicating to Peter, "Ah, you almost made it!"

Doubt is certainly an element of the life of faith, and God is looking for people who are ready to follow him through those moments of uncertainty; for when we come through those moments of doubt, we come out stronger on the other end. Will you finish the "race" of faith to the finish line? Will you persevere in the midst of times of doubt and uncertainty that face all who follow Jesus?

PRAY

Jesus, after my encounter with you, I am confident of your love for me, no matter what happens in my life. During those times when doubt may enter my life, allow me the grace to move forward, knowing that you are present. Amen.

CONTEMPLATE

"Don't expect faith to clear things up for you. It is trust, not certainty."

Flannery O'Connor

WONDER

1. When has your trust in another person been betrayed? How did it feel?
2. How does knowledge of Jesus provide comfort in times of uncertainty?
3. In what ways does "faith" become active when we move forward in times of doubt?

FOUR

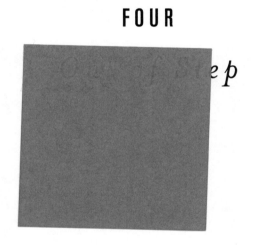

Out of Step

16

LORD, WHEN DID WE SEE YOU HUNGRY AND FEED YOU, OR THIRSTY AND GIVE YOU DRINK?

Matthew 25:37

In February of 2013, I had a book published that is titled *Jesus the Evangelist: A Gospel Guide to the New Evangelization*. The premise was that while there is no perfect program in evangelization, there is the perfect person: Jesus Christ. A month after it came out, my wife and I attended a St. Patrick's Day celebration and dinner at a neighboring parish. The school gymnasium was transformed into a sea of green, and our ears were treated to authentic Irish Gaelic music straight from the lungs of one of our friends, a native son of Ireland. His calming yet powerful voice has the ability to transport one across the Atlantic, to the rolling hills and sphagnum moss of the rugged countryside of the Emerald Isle, and arouse the voices of long-dead Irish writers, playwrights, and poets that echo from the soil. It is soothing to the soul.

While some school children were entertaining the crowd with traditional Irish dancing, I was making my second, maybe third, trip to the carving station, pretending, of course, that it was my first time there, as the turkey, roast beef, and steak were thinly sliced and piled high on my plate. My plate was overflowing, but I was trying to pace myself, knowing full well that if the food was this sumptuous, the desserts must be lavish, too.

I had mentioned more than once, quite casually, to anyone who would listen (from the pastor on down) that my latest book had just come out with all the false humility I could muster. I, of course, was more than willing to share my deep insights and profound theological knowledge with anyone with ears on the topic of evangelization and, more specifically, the topic of yours truly.

As we sat at our round table with two or three other couples, my wife, who was to my left, grabbed my arm and said softly, "I'll be right back." She rose, placed her napkin on the seat and proceeded to walk over to a woman sitting by herself at another table directly in front of me, not twenty feet away. My wife smiled as she bent down and asked the woman, "Would you like to sit with us?" The woman looked up, gave a big smile, and said, "Oh thank you, thank you! I would love that!" The woman came to our table and joined us for the meal as my wife picked up her napkin and returned to her seat without a word.

While I was the one who had written a book about evangelization, endorsed by both a cardinal and a bishop, it was my wife who was the expert evangelist. She put the twenty-three chapters I had written into one humble, spontaneous act of loving service and invitation without any fanfare. I can't recall anything else I said that evening, but I will never forget my wife's loving action toward a woman who sat alone at a parish function, directly in front of me, whom I had neglected to see.

It was Pope Paul VI who wrote that "the people of our day are more impressed by witnesses than by teachers, and if they listen to these it is because they also bear witness" (*Evangelii Nuntiandi*, 19). Our life in Christ must bear fruit in our actions as we continue to grow in faith and mature in obedience. St. James states, "Faith without works is useless" (Jas 2:20).

Lord, When Did We See You Hungry and Feed You, or Thirsty and Give You Drink?

Jesus gives us a foreshadowing of the final judgment that will come to all people. It's in this story that the question is posed by Jesus through a person who is *righteous* (virtuous, honorable, or blameless) and enters the kingdom of Heaven.

"Lord, when did we see you hungry and feed you, or thirsty and give you drink?

The answer given is, "Amen, I say to you, whatever you did for one of these least brothers of mine, you did for me" (Mt 25:40).

As we allow the Holy Spirit to transform us from within, the fruit of that interior conversion must be evident in our actions toward others. Not because others are Catholic but because we are. As with my own poor example of charity while at the St. Patrick's Day dinner with my wife, there will be missed opportunities, times when we just blow it due to selfishness and sin. The hope is that as we mature in faith, those missed opportunities will become fewer and fewer and we can echo the words of St. Paul, "It is no longer I who live but Christ who lives in me" (Gal 2:20). The important thing is to continue to grow in our knowledge of the faith so, as we grow, our actions of *Christlike* love and joyful service will flow naturally as a way of life and not as a forced imperative.

Who are the hungry, the thirsty in your life? Who is the stranger, the imprisoned, the naked, or the sick where you live and work? You don't need to travel very far to find people who are lacking these most basic needs. It was St. Teresa of Calcutta who advised that if you can't feed one hundred people, feed one. Who is that one person you can serve today? Pray, ask God to open your eyes and to use you, for he is not concerned with your ability but with your availability.

The Church has always had an eye for the poor and the marginalized from the beginning of its existence. There are countless organizations within the Catholic Church and religious orders with the sole purpose of caring for our brothers and sisters in need.

St. Teresa of Calcutta also noted that when you give a hungry person in India a piece of bread, you have satiated his hunger, yet in the wealthy countries the poverty goes much deeper. We have an ample supply of the basic necessities of life, but we have a great hunger for love, which can hardly be satiated by a piece of bread. We also have many, many people in our society who feel isolated, unloved, and alone. The material goods we have offer a poor substitute for what they really need. When we reach out to them, we are putting our love for God in concrete action.

Who have you reached out to because of Christ's words? What opportunities await you? And will you put your love for God in action?

PRAY

Jesus, thank you for the faith that you have given me. I pray that I will let your words and the example you gave guide me in all things. Forgive me for the times I have neglected others and even looked down on them instead of reaching out to them in charity. With your help, I'll do better. Amen.

CONTEMPLATE

"At the end of life we will not be judged by how many diplomas we have received, how much money we have made, how many great things we have done. We will be judged by 'I was hungry, and you gave me something to eat, I was naked and you clothed me. I was homeless, and you took me in.'"

St. Teresa of Calcutta

WONDER

1. Was there a time when you were humbled by the caring actions of another, actions directed either toward you or toward someone else?
2. Think of a time when you missed the mark and failed to take advantage of an opportunity to serve. What might you do differently now?
3. Have you ever intentionally served another who was hungry, sick, homeless, or imprisoned? What was the experience like?
4. Who is your best witness to Christ?

17

IS A LAMP BROUGHT IN TO BE PLACED UNDER A BUSHEL BASKET OR UNDER A BED, AND NOT TO BE PLACED ON A LAMPSTAND?

Mark 4:21

Like many people, I'm passionate about sports and follow my teams religiously. Unfortunately, the teams I root for seem to win championships every twenty to thirty years. When my teams win, I'm ecstatic and the thrill of victory lasts a couple of years; then follow years of mild sports depression.

You can accuse me of being many things, but being unfaithful to my teams is not one of them. In season or out, I wear the shirts and hats, proudly displaying my allegiance. I'm not a bandwagon guy who only pulls out the shirts when they win; in a sense, my allegiance is up "on a lampstand" for all to see. My children also wear the logos in patient expectation like their dad, who is forever hopeful that *this year* will be *the year* and a championship may occur in their lifetime.

In Mark chapter 4, Jesus teaches the crowds along the shores of the Sea of Galilee. They are pressing in on him in order to hear his words. He retreats alone and is then approached by his twelve apostles and a few others for clarification about his teaching. It is here, in the privacy of his

inner circle, that he asks the question, "Is a lamp brought in
to be placed under a bushel basket or under a bed, and not
to be placed on a lampstand?"

While the obvious answer is no, there is more than meets
the eye to this simple admonition. In Jesus' day, ordinary
lamps were made from clay. They were simple, with a res-
ervoir for the olive oil and a "nozzle" on which the flax wick
would rest. Household lamps were small enough to be carried in the palm of the hand and easy to hold while navi-
gating in the dark. The higher the lamp was held, the more
it illuminated the room or path.

The Hebrew word used for "lamp," however, denotes any
kind of candle, lamp, or torch that is used to illuminate the
way or room. For the listeners of Jesus' day, the immediate
connection was not a traditional lamp or large flashlight
that a person might use while camping on a scouting trip
today. In Judaism, there are significant uses for the candle
and deep religious traditions associated with lampstands
that are worth reflecting on, for they would have most likely
been in the minds of those gathered around Jesus.

One use for a candle that was familiar to all Jews was for
proper observance of the Sabbath in which a candle was lit
and placed on a lampstand or menorah before sundown on
Friday evening in every Jewish home. It marked the beginning of the Sabbath or Shabbat, the Jewish day of rest. The
threefold purpose was to commemorate God's creation of
the universe with God's rest on the seventh day, to celebrate
the Israelites' redemption from slavery in Egypt, and to fore-
shadow *Olam Haba*, or the Messianic age, when peace and
brotherhood would rule. This set the Jewish people apart

from their contemporaries, and it reminded Jewish families of God's actions in salvation history.

Another significant correlation may be with the great Jewish Feast of Tabernacles or Sukkoth. At end of the first day of the feast, the Temple in Jerusalem was gloriously illuminated by gigantic candelabras. Each of the four golden candelabras is said to have been about seventy-five feet tall. Each had four branches, and at the top of every branch, there was a large golden bowl. Four young rabbinic students, bearing pitchers of oil, would climb ladders to fill the four golden bowls on each candelabra. And then the oil in those bowls was ignited. Imagine sixteen golden lamps blazing upward, soaring toward the desert sky and visible from miles away. The light was to remind the people of how God's glory had once filled his Temple, and it was said that the light illuminated every inch of the city as the noonday sun.

It was at this feast that Jesus exclaimed, "I am the light of the world. Whoever follows me will never walk in darkness, but will have the light of life" (Jn 8:12). In the person of Jesus, God's glory was once again present in that Temple; he used the backdrop of the celebration to announce that reality. Just as Jesus replaced the Temple and became God's dwelling among us, so, too, he calls his followers to shine with the presence of God and to let that light be visible to all.

This message of Jesus must not be hidden or kept private, for there are no closet Catholics. Rather, our faith must be lived out loud, proclaimed openly and clearly in order that those who encounter us may encounter Christ in us. The love we have for one another, the hope that sustains us, and the Spirit who empowers us are to be shared with others that they, too, might become children of God. Jesus instructs his disciples to proclaim the message of God's love, mercy, and forgiveness that they have received.

Is a Lamp Brought in to Be Placed under a Bushel Basket or under a Bed, and Not to Be Placed on a Lampstand?

The early Christians were expelled from the synagogues, and history records the martyrdom of many believers who refused to deny Christ. Yet today, as in Jesus' day, disciples are still tempted to do otherwise for a number of reasons, most of which have to do with fear: fear that we may be persecuted for our beliefs; fear of being labeled by family, friends, coworkers, or society as out-of-touch with modern, politically correct thinking; fear of ridicule; and fear that our newfound faith may negatively impact our businesses or careers.

What's holding you back from expressing your faith in Jesus and communion with his Church? How will you live your life? Will you constantly gauge and evaluate the waters of political correctness, keeping quiet due to fear, or will you articulate your encounter with Jesus with ease, enthusiasm, and joy? Pope Francis noted, "There are more witnesses, more martyrs in the Church today than there were in the first centuries. It begins with witness, day after day, and it can end like Jesus, the first martyr, the first witness, the faithful witness: with blood."[13]

Those who have never encountered Jesus may not read the Bible, but they do read Christians. Your behavior, your witness in good times and bad, is constantly on display for the non-Christian world as is mine. What are you communicating about Jesus verbally and non-verbally? Faith is communicated through relationships, so our witness must be lived authentically through our actions and our words to all we encounter, believers or not.

Yes, I'm extremely faithful to my sports teams, and win or lose, I'm not afraid to associate myself with them. Yet my encounter with Jesus Christ and living witness through both word and action is infinitely more important than whether my teams do well. Following Jesus means that our witness must be firm; we must have faith in Jesus but also the faith of Jesus, who entrusted everything to God's mercy, to his Father's will.

Pray, study the scriptures, grow in faith, and let your light shine before all the world, which is desperate for the truth.

PRAY

Lord Jesus, I am inspired by the witness of so many Christians around the world who give their lives as martyrs in witness to their faith in you. May I never be ashamed or fearful to let others know I believe in you and entrust my life to your care. Support me with others who are strong in faith, and strengthen me through your Word and the sacraments. Amen.

CONTEMPLATE

"You meet certain people, you have contact with certain persons or places, your life has a certain circumscription, God overshadowing and intervening in all. This is called your daily providence. Like the skin on your face it is yours personally, nobody else ever had it, nobody else ever will have it. Every one of us is the center of a particular bit of

Divine Providence. How can we get people to realize that in their everyday providence they are the Catholic Church; that they are responsible for the Church, that they should act for the Church, be vigilant for her interests and plead her cause? How, in a word, can we effect that every Catholic, no matter in what circumstances he may be, will be a missionary?"

Fr. Thomas A. Judge, C.M.

WONDER

1. Think about sports teams, favorite vacation spots, or perhaps restaurants that you speak of frequently. Do you speak about them with the same ease you speak about your faith?
2. Who has provided a good witness to faith in your own life?
3. What fears, real or imagined, do you have concerning letting your faith be known by others?
4. What can help you overcome your fear and encourage you to live your faith courageously in the world?

18

WHICH OF THESE THREE, IN YOUR OPINION, WAS NEIGHBOR TO THE ROBBER'S VICTIM?

Luke 10:36

In a simple Google search of the phrase "Good Samaritan," well over twelve million results pop up on the computer screen in less than one second. Even those who have little or no religious background are at least vaguely familiar with this parable of Jesus and its main idea, which is helping those who can't help themselves.

As disciples of Jesus, we are called to help those in need—not because they are Christians but because *we are*. The point of the story may seem simple, yet there are certainly layers to this parable of Jesus that are worth examining from a first century, Middle Eastern point of view. The details of this parable, which are often overlooked, were remembered and recorded by the early Christian community, so they must be important. As we continue our journey of faith in Jesus and grow as mature Christians, let's consider these details before we reflect on this crucial question of Jesus, "Which of these three, in your opinion, was neighbor to the robber's victim?"

Jesus tells this parable of the Good Samaritan in response to a lawyer who puts a question to Jesus in order to test him.

The lawyer stands up and says to Jesus, "Teacher, what must I do to inherit eternal life?" (Lk 10:25). Standing up is a sign of respect in the Middle East, and the lawyer addresses Jesus with a respectful title, "teacher." We should not be too harsh in our judgment of this lawyer when we read the phrase, "*to test him*," for this is the way a person discerns if a teacher has any wisdom in that culture. We see others asking Jesus questions throughout the New Testament, and even in the Old Testament, we find the Queen of Sheba testing Solomon: "The queen of Sheba, having heard a report of Solomon's fame, came to test him with subtle questions" (1 Kgs 10:1).

One thing that is true of lawyers from two thousand years ago in Jerusalem and at a large firm in New York City today: a lawyer *never* asks a question without already knowing the answer. So what's going on here in this story? Is this lawyer a sincere seeker of truth or someone seeking to justify his behavior? This lawyer is in the midst of a crowd and asks a question to which he already sort of knows the answer. Most likely he assumes that Jesus will tell him what he must do according to the Torah, and he can affirm publicly, in the sight of everyone, that yes, indeed, he is doing all of these things. The question itself seems a bit odd since the lawyer knows that there really is nothing he can *do* to inherit eternal life. Eternal life is a gift that can't be earned in the proper sense; it's a gift to be received.

Jesus begins a discussion on the law but first asks the questioner about his opinion. Jesus asks, "What is written in the law? How do you read it?" (Lk 10:26). Jesus knows that the lawyer will affirm the law; the man masterfully begins to quote from Deuteronomy 6:5 (on love of God) and Leviticus 19:18 (on love of neighbor). Jesus responds with praise and a challenge: "Do this and you will live" (Lk 10:28). This law-yer has the right theology, *but* is he willing to *act* on it? The lawyer asks a question about eternal life, and Jesus expands the conversation to include *all* life. The Greek word for "live" used here by Jesus carries the connotation of *do this and you will come alive, you will be living*. This is a direct quote from the Old Testament character Joseph found in Genesis 42:18 as Joseph addresses his brothers. Joseph is talking about the present, not a future event. The word translated as *do* is in the imperative in the Greek translation, where it means *keep on doing*.

The lawyer who asked a specific question concerning what he can do to inherit eternal life is now challenged to keep on doing this, loving God and loving neighbor contin-ually, day and night, and then he will *come alive*. But who can love God and neighbor *all the time*? It's becoming clear to the lawyer that this standard is too high, yet he still desires to do something to see himself fully righteous and gain the praise of Jesus and those who are listening to this conversation.

From the lawyer's next question, in verse 29, we gather that he knows the God whom he must love, for God has revealed himself to Israel and through the scripture. How to love God is not his question but, rather, how to love his neighbor: "And who is my neighbor?" (Remember, lawyers never ask a question without already knowing the answer.) This lawyer was no doubt familiar with Leviticus 19:17–18, which identifies the neighbor as being one's brother and the sons of one's own people; basically, this included all Jews. Scholars of the day were divided as to whether converts or proselytes were neighbors, and they definitely agreed that Gentiles were not neighbors.[14] Scripture scholar Joachim

Jeremias mentions that rabbinic literature around the time of Jesus stated that "heretics, informers, and renegades should be pushed into the ditch and not pulled out."[15]

It is after this dialogue that Jesus tells the parable of the Good Samaritan. The road that stretches from Jerusalem to Jericho, on which this parable is set, is seventeen miles long and is one of the most dangerous roads in all the Middle East. Jerusalem sits about 2,300 feet *above* sea level and Jericho sits 1,700 feet *below* sea level, so each step of the way descending from Jerusalem becomes hotter and more difficult to travel and navigate. It was common knowledge that robbers would attack people on this road, so traveling in a group or caravan was the way to go.

Each word of this parable is carefully crafted by Jesus in order to bring the question of "Who is my neighbor?" to light. We are told that a man fell among robbers, was stripped, beaten, and left half-dead. The fact that the man fell among robbers was no surprise to the original listeners, but the fact that he traveled alone would have raised an eyebrow; everyone would know that this man was foolish for doing do. We learn that he was stripped of clothing. In the Middle East of Jesus' day, as it is today, clothes reveal a person's identity. Jews, Romans, Greeks and others all had distinctive styles of clothing. In fact, Jews were commanded by God to wear certain types of clothing to remind them of the covenant. A quick view of any ancient frescoes and paintings reveal that each culture had its particular customs of dress. In this parable, we can't discern nor see the man's clothes, which would have provided some clue as to his identity. His religion? His country of origin? He is stripped of these outward clues; we only know that he's a human being in need.

The fact that he was beaten and half-dead leads us to believe that he may have put up a struggle with the robbers and therefore would have been left bleeding and unconscious. Jewish rabbis were ritually forbidden to have contact with a corpse. According to the written law, touching a corpse was number one on the list of sources of defilement. According to the oral law of the time period, contact with a non-Jew was forbidden and made a rabbi unclean or defiled.

Which of These Three, in Your Opinion, Was Neighbor to the Robber's Victim?

When we look at the movement of the three people going down the same road, perhaps we can have not only some sympathy for the victim but also a new understanding from the point of view of the priest and the Levite. It would be unjust to characterize the actions of the priest and Levite as uncaring or indifferent from their unspoken rulebook. The movement of the priest going down this road signals to the reader that he has just completed his priestly service in Jerusalem at the Temple. In most cases, this service lasted two weeks out of the year, when he would have officiated at the daily Temple rituals. The Levite would have assisted the priest.

If the priest were to touch a Gentile or a person stained with blood, he would have made himself ritually impure (see Numbers 19). This would have meant going back up to Jerusalem and having to perform the rites of cleansing for a priest, which included obtaining a red heifer and reducing it to ashes; this ritual would have lasted a full week. In addition to this, imagine the humiliation he would have endured if he was ritually impure. It would have mean that during the daily offering, he would have had to publicly place himself at the Eastern gate during the time of sacrifice and announce himself as unclean.

As the priest is going down the road and he sees this stripped and beaten man, he has a decision to make. *Will I get involved in this man's life? I don't know if he is a Jew. He may already be dead. I think I see blood on his person.* The idea of being publicly disgraced, shamed, and humiliated in the Temple among his peers does not seem appealing. He wants to keep himself ritually pure. The faithful Jews who hear the story will empathize with him and applaud his decision not to get involved and defile himself.

The same scenario is contemplated by the Levite, who doesn't go to the other side but comes a little closer to the place. He most likely knows that the priest did not get involved and thinks to himself, *If the priest didn't stop to help, why should I stop?* While the harsh restrictions that applied to priests did not apply to Levites, those faithful to the Law will nod in approval at this man's actions.

The priest goes to the other side.

The Levite goes to the place.

The Samaritan goes to the person.

It's the compassionate actions of the Samaritan, completed in silence, which set the example for loving neighbor. The Samaritan offers the first aid that the priest and Levite failed to provide. He asks no questions as to the nationality of this wounded man. He seeks no sign of what religion the man professes or tribe that he attaches himself to. He doesn't ask a litany of questions to see if the man's theology is like his own. He doesn't withhold mercy because of the man's foolish decision to travel alone. All the Samaritan sees is a fellow human being in need, and that is enough to evoke compassion.

The care the Samaritan gives uses familiar biblical language of "binding up wounds" and "pouring oil and wine." These are the actions of God in Jeremiah 30:17: "For I will restore your health; I will heal your injuries." While the priest and Levite poured out the offerings to God in the Temple, it is the Samaritan who now pours out the acceptable sacrifice that God calls for in responding to this man's need. The Samaritan takes this one step further. Robbers take money from this man; the Samaritan provides what the robbers seized in paying for his extended stay at the inn.

Jesus turns to the lawyer and asks a question: "Which of these three, in your opinion, was neighbor to the robber's victim?" Jesus asks the question that forces the lawyer to consider: *Toward whom must I become a neighbor?*

The lawyer responds correctly, "The one who treated him with mercy." Jesus, in responding to the lawyer, who wants to *do* something in order to inherit eternal life, says "Go and *do* likewise" (Lk 10:37, emphasis added).

On our own spiritual journey, we cannot *inherit* eternal life. It comes to us as a gift, and our response is the quality of mercy we show to others. This is the standard we are called to strive for. We must put love into action. Obtaining theological degrees, reading the gospels, studying the *Catechism of the Catholic Church*, and giving proper respect at liturgy are inconsequential if they fail to help us become more loving and compassionate to anyone in need, even an enemy.

PRAY

Lord Jesus, what you ask is often beyond my power. Loving those who hate me, showing mercy and compassion to those who may not even realize my sacrifice, and caring for people who get in trouble by their own foolish behaviors is a new way of living for me. Stir your Holy Spirit within me; let me see as you see and love as you love, without counting the cost. Amen.

CONTEMPLATE

"I really only love God as much as I love the person I love least."

Dorothy Day

WONDER

1. Have you ever experienced being left behind, forgotten, or ignored? How did it feel? How did it impact you? Did the experience make you bitter or better?
2. Why do we place so much emphasis on the outward appearance of people? Has a person's outward appearance ever been a reason for your refusal to approach them?
3. The priest went to the other side of the injured man while the Samaritan went to the person. How may this fact challenge your call to be like Christ?
4. What opportunities and challenges do you face after reflecting on this question?

19

WHAT MAN AMONG YOU HAVING A HUNDRED SHEEP AND LOSING ONE OF THEM WOULD NOT LEAVE THE NINETY-NINE IN THE DESERT AND GO AFTER THE LOST ONE UNTIL HE FINDS IT?

Luke 15:4

One lost sheep may not be a big deal to you or me. After all, of the ninety-nine sheep that are together, the one lost sheep amounts to one percent of the whole, which to some is statistically insignificant. However, when we realize that this shepherd is entrusted with one hundred sheep that belong to the community, things change. If your family entrusts four sheep to the shepherd and one goes missing, well then, that percentage rises to twenty-five percent of one family's sheep and that *is* significant. The Middle Eastern village of Jesus' time is a close-knit community, so when one family suffers, everyone must sacrifice to make up for what is lacking in another's family. Yes, one sheep is of value to this good shepherd. No matter how lost it may be, the sheep retains its value in his eyes.

Jesus asks this question to the religious leaders of his time in such a way that the question begs an affirmative answer: "Of course we would go after the lost one until we find it." Jesus then teaches by way of this parable as a means of defending his own behavior of eating meals with and reaching out to sinners. In reality, Jesus is saying something along the lines of "You're upset because I'm eating with tax collectors and sinners? It's worse than you think! I'm not only eating with them . . . I'm seeking them out!"

The religious leadership at the time of Jesus was greatly offended by his choice of companions: sinners, prostitutes, and tax collectors, all people who wanted to find God but were never given that opportunity by the religious establishment. We see the love of God on display in the pages of the gospels and especially in Jesus' concern for those who are on the margins: the forgotten, sick, lonely, and the broad category of "sinners." While we are all sinners and have fallen short of God's desire for perfection or holiness, it's plain to see that the "in-crowd"—those who strictly abided by the precepts of the Mosaic Law—felt that having a meal and table fellowship with those who were considered outsiders should be avoided at the very least.

We find this desire to separate from others in many walks of life that cut across cultures and time. Members of the in-crowd view themselves as different from and naturally superior to others. Pride rushes in, and those outsiders are looked down upon. Perhaps the in-crowd has special knowledge or has undergone training in secret that sets them apart and, in their minds, above others. While there are certainly experiences and situations in which we will feel naturally inclined to be with certain people, the Gospel message is clear that we are all God's children and are all created in the image and likeness of God (see *CCC*, 1700).

As disciples of Jesus Christ, we who believe join together with other Christians in our worship, study, prayer, and acts of service. Like Jesus, we don't withdraw from the world in disgust; rather, we offer the costly love of Jesus to the world, which means offering it to those who may not even know Jesus. It involves reaching out to those who are lost, those on the margins of society, whatever that may look like in your community. Our job is to love, to inform, and to witness to others about Jesus.

Some of the earliest depictions of Jesus in early Christian history are not of the Crucifixion but of the shepherd carrying a lost sheep back to the community over his shoulders. That image continues to inspire people to reflect on how Jesus has both rescued us and restored us to good favor with God. It also reminds us of our responsibility to follow Jesus' example.

What Man among You Having a Hundred Sheep and Losing One of Them Would Not Leave the Ninety-Nine in the Desert and Go After the Lost One Until He Finds It?

As with most change and conversions in life, the first step is a renewal of our minds, conforming ours to the mind of Jesus and his Church. St. Paul writes to the Corinthian community that "we have the mind of Christ" (1 Cor 2:16) and again to the Romans, "Do not conform yourselves to this age but be transformed by the renewal of your mind, that you may discern what is the will of God, what is good and pleasing and perfect" (Rom 12:2). Having the mind of Christ is possible because Jesus has sent us his Holy Spirit, who dwells in us to guide and empower us for witness.

Do we have eyes and ears for those who are lost? They may be in the wilderness, or they may be right in our own homes. They may be financially poor, without clean clothes, or they may be driving new vehicles and living in luxurious estates.

In Jesus' parable, the seeking shepherd leaves the ninety-nine and ventures out into the wilderness to seek the lost sheep. When a sheep is separated from the flock, a few things happen. First off, when the sheep realizes he is separated, he becomes petrified and won't move an inch due to fear. The sheep will then do two things that will put the animal in grave danger. It will make a loud "bleating" sound, and then the sheep, out of fear, will urinate on itself. Not a pretty picture, I know. These actions will make the lost sheep easy prey for the predators nearby. Both birds of prey from above and four legged predators will hear the distressed cries and pick up on the scent of the animal and know they have an easy meal.

The shepherd is well aware of this, and so he places himself in harm's way, alone in the wilderness, not immune from the predators himself, all for the sake of one lost sheep. Jesus remarks in the parable that this shepherd places the soiled sheep on his shoulders "with joy."

In this parable of the Lost Sheep or Seeking Shepherd, attention is given to the one that is lost. Not the whole herd; just one lost sheep. The shepherd will demonstrate unexpected love in seeking out the lost one, a behavior we are expected to model in reaching out to others.

As your faith matures, as you develop the mind of Christ, will you follow in the master's footsteps and imitate his example in reaching out to the lost?

PRAY

Jesus, thank you for rescuing me and for restoring me to yourself and your Church. May I never forget what it was to be lost and separated from your love and to be found by you. May the same mercy I received from you compel me to tell others of your love and the Good News. May my ears, eyes, and heart be open to reaching out to others as you did, in love. Amen.

CONTEMPLATE

"The joy of the Church is to give birth; the joy of the Church is to go out of herself to give life; the joy of the Church is go out and seek the sheep that are lost; the joy of the Church is precisely the tenderness of the shepherd, the tenderness of the mother."

Pope Francis

WONDER

1. So much of Jesus' ministry focuses on one person at a time. Is there a temptation to desire big crowds and yet ignore the individual?
2. How can you *hear* and *see* if a person may be lost?
3. What may be the *cost* of your seeking the lost?
4. What *joy* is associated with seeking the lost?

20

CAN YOU DRINK THE CUP
THAT I AM GOING TO DRINK?

Matthew 20:22

During my twenty-plus years as a teacher, hundreds of wonderful students passed through my classroom. I can honestly say I loved every minute of it, with rare exceptions. Many positive things happened during the fifty minutes of class time, and while I pray that I was faithful in communicating the Good News of Jesus to every student who came through my door, the one activity I enjoyed the most took place outside of class time: table tennis!

Before school, during lunch periods, in between periods, and after school, students would gather around the two game tables, eager to try their hands at a quick match to seven or, when time allowed, twenty-one points. We had bumper stickers with the phrase "Feel the Wrath" emblazoned on them and shirts with the same phrase that members of the club would wear under their school uniforms. We had individual handcrafted bats or paddles, each with the particular type of wood and desired thickness of rubber specifically designed for the style of play. They were kept in individual cases lest they be damaged.

Each year standouts would be invited to be on the Court of Elders, students who ensured the proper playing of the game, knew the terminology, and excelled at the sport. A number of club members would join together with me at the New Jersey Table Tennis Club in Westfield, where we would play against others in a Monday-night league.

A tradition that grew out of the Monday night league was the trip to the local diner afterward. The friendships and bonding that formed around the ping-pong table were reinforced and strengthened over meals at the diner. The same songs were played on the jukebox and the same meals were ordered after every league night.

Each student's grade point average would decline in direct proportion to the amount of time spent in the table tennis room, but no one seemed to mind, and they are all now successful men and women who I hope attribute their current success to their time spent playing table tennis.

Remembering those times still brings a smile to my face, and reconnecting with the students after all those years reminds me that game time was not wasted time. (OK, maybe some time was wasted.) Those ordinary things of life that are experienced together have a way of forging memories, uniting all who participate. Whether it's after-school club meetings, athletic competitions, or military training, those who go through the experience know the connection, the bond that outsiders can't relate to.

In our decision to follow Jesus, we will have opportunities to bond together through sharing in the cup of suffering. The road of discipleship, of following Jesus, leads to the Cross. There's no way around it. You can't avoid it or pray your way out of it. It's a stumbling block for many, but those who pick up their crosses and embrace them while following Jesus find that their faith becomes perfected, Christlike.

Can You Drink the Cup
That I Am Going to Drink?

Jesus' words are more of a challenge than a question posed to his two closest disciples. They saw the miraculous, heard his preaching, experienced the massive crowds that were following, and witnessed Jesus transfigured before their eyes. It's no wonder the two disciples want to follow him. The allure of power and prestige; that desire to *be* someone, to be known, to be popular; and the possibility that all earthly yearnings will be fulfilled—everyone wants that. The disciples are not excluded.

Jesus' reference to the cup evokes his prayer as he prepares to be arrested: "take this cup away from me" (Mk 14:36). In fact, in Matthew's account, Jesus prays this prayer three times (Mt 26:39, 42, 44). Jesus also associates drinking the cup to his passion in Mark 10:38–39 in his response to the request of James and John to sit at his right and left in the coming kingdom.

In the Old Testament, the image of the cup is used to symbolize suffering (Ps 75:9) and judgment (Is 51:17, 22; Jer 25:15–29; 49:12; Lam 4:21; Ez 23:31–34; Hb 2:16). While the request to sit at Jesus' left and right in the kingdom originates from their mother, the two disciples are present and answer Jesus' question concerning "drinking from the cup" in the affirmative. They respond, "We can" (Mt 20:22).

At another time, Jesus tells his disciples that they must deny themselves, take up their cross, and follow him. Jesus' passion, death, and resurrection is central to his life and will be to the lives and mission of his disciples, too. Yet despite their initial confidence, the disciples would falter, and their initial enthusiasm would wane when confronted with the scourging, beating, and crucifixion of Jesus. It's difficult to face the cross let alone embrace it.

We are reminded again of the cup, the cup of the New Covenant, at the Last Supper when Jesus says, "Drink from it, all of you; for this is my blood of the covenant, which will be shed on behalf of many for the forgiveness of sins" (Mt 26:27–28). Our sacramental participation in the New Covenant is expressed emphatically by sharing in the cup because blood is the central sign of covenant.

Where does that leave you? If you're looking for an escape from suffering through Christianity, look elsewhere, for you won't find it here. If you're looking for a "prosperity theology" that promises wealth, health, and happiness by declaring yourself a follower of Jesus, you're in for a rude awakening. If you're looking for meaning in suffering and the strength to carry the crosses that will come your way, then you're in the right place.

In the same way we are united with Christ in our sufferings, Catholics are fortunate to have a long list of saints who show us the way and who remained faithful in the midst of their suffering. One of the most beloved and heroic saints who endured suffering was St. Thérèse of Lisieux, a French woman who joined a religious order called the Carmelites. In a letter to her sister Céline, St. Thérèse of Lisieux wrote, "I know quite well all you are suffering. I know your anguish, and I share it. Oh! If I could but impart to you the peace which Jesus has put into my soul amid my most bitter tears. Be comforted—all passes away."[16]

The "peace which Jesus has put into my soul" is a glimpse into the life of a saint who knew the agony of illness and died of tuberculosis at the age of twenty-four. Her life and the lives of many of the saints and suffering Christians embraced the cross God had for them through the power of the Holy Spirit. They truly witnessed to God's love in the midst of their suffering.

What life will bring our way is certainly unknown, but we are confident that, good or bad, Christ walks with us each step of the way. He will provide us the strength, fortitude, and grace needed to endure any and all crosses. He will provide a way for our faith to shine in the midst of the darkness. Yes, we will endure suffering in various forms, but in doing so, we will also encounter Jesus and his eternal love.

Will you have the faith and courage to share in the sufferings of Jesus? Will you stand by him in his trials? Will you drink from his cup?

PRAY

Lord Jesus, you suffered for me, and I will joyfully follow you even to the Cross. Increase my faith and joy in the midst of suffering, and allow me the grace to embrace whatever crosses come my way. Give me an eye to assist those who are carrying burdens so I may imitate you in love. Amen.

CONTEMPLATE

"Lent brought on new meaning in my life as I was brought closer to Our Lord through experiencing sufferings which in small ways I could relate to his own Passion. But at the same time, spiritual desolation crept in making me feel so alone and far from God. I would try to cry out to him in these times, 'Jesus, I love you so much!' The feeling didn't change, but I knew in my mind that God was with me. He is always with us and is bringing about good no matter what it may seem like—we must remember this. I try to trust that God has even bigger and more beautiful plans for me—that his plans are better than mine—and that every human life is a gift. Jesus I trust in you!"

Michelle Duppong

WONDER

1. How do you respond to suffering or difficult situations?
2. Have you ever "blamed" God for suffering in your life?
3. How do faith and the Cross bring meaning to our suffering and trials?
4. What "crosses" have you had to bear in your life so far, and how have you carried them?

FIVE

The Anchor

21

WHERE IS THE GUEST ROOM WHERE I MAY EAT THE PASSOVER WITH MY DISCIPLES?

Luke 22:11

Isn't it true that some of life's most memorable moments happen without our realizing their significance at the time? The joyful memories of time spent with family and relatives as a child, the daily routine of eating with friends at the school cafeteria, participating in activities with our friends at college before we head our separate ways, or the last encounter with a loved one who unexpectedly dies shortly afterward can occur without our recognizing their significance.

I remember vividly the last time I went out for dinner at the Myersville Inn with Steve, a former student who became one of my closest friends. We attended countless hockey and basketball games at Madison Square Garden together, and along with another friend, Shawn, had season tickets the year the New York Rangers won the Stanley Cup. There was never a trip to Atlantic City or Keansburg down the Jersey Shore that Steve wasn't ready to take at a moment's notice, nor was there a ticket to a Yankees game or a Billy Joel concert that he couldn't get his hands on. Out of the blue, he was diagnosed with cancer, and it had metastasized aggressively throughout his body. I knew that he was weak and had lost a considerable amount of weight, but it was an extraordinary experience to assist him from the car to the steps of the restaurant and then to our table. Little did I know then that it would be the last time we would share a meal together.

We can all look back and say to some degree, "I wish I would have appreciated that time more" or "I wish I would have let those people know how much they meant to me." If we're fortunate, we can plan ahead when we sense a special occasion is at hand or special people are present so we can soak up every minute.

The celebration of the Last Supper, the Passover meal, was one such event that was well-anticipated by Jesus. One could say it had been foreseen even before the creation of the world.

As Catholics, the celebration of the Eucharist is "the source and summit of Christian life" (*Lumen Gentium*, 11). What happened on Calvary, where Jesus was crucified, is that Jesus offered himself to God the Father for our salvation. In the celebration of the Eucharist, this same sacrifice of Christ, made once for all historically, is present here and now sacramentally and celebrated on the altar. We can say this because Jesus, who was both priest who *offered* and victim who *was offered*, is present here and now in the Eucharist. In this way, the "work of our redemption is accomplished" through his Eucharistic offering, and fruits of Christ's unique sacrifice are applied to us here and now (see *CCC*, 1366).

Where Is the Guest Room Where I May Eat the Passover with My Disciples?

The Last Supper of Jesus was a Passover meal. This meal is enormously significant for a Jewish person, for it recalls the event of the Exodus and the Passover of the Lord when the Hebrew people were liberated from their slavery in Egypt. The significance for Christians lies in the fact that at this Passover meal, Jesus transformed the bread and wine into his Body and Blood and shared it with his disciples: "While they were eating, Jesus took bread, said the blessing, broke it, and giving it to his disciples said, 'Take and eat; this is my body.' Then he took a cup, gave thanks, and gave it to them, saying, 'Drink from it, all of you, for this is my blood of the covenant, which will be shed on behalf of many for the forgiveness of sins'" (Mt 26:26–28; see also Mk 14:22–24, Lk 22:17–20, 1 Cor 11:23–25).

The Catholic Church professes that, in the celebration of the Eucharist, bread and wine become the Body and Blood of Jesus Christ through the power of the Holy Spirit and the instrumentality of the priest. Jesus said, "I am the living bread that came down from heaven; whoever eats this bread will live forever; and the bread that I will give is my flesh for the life of the world. . . . For my flesh is true food, and my blood is true drink" (Jn 6:51–55). The whole Christ is truly present, body, blood, soul, and divinity, under the appearances of bread and wine—the glorified Christ who rose from the dead after dying for our sins. This is what the Church means when she speaks of the "Real Presence" of Christ in the Eucharist. This presence of Christ in the Eucharist is not called "real" to exclude other types of his presence as if they could not be understood as real (see *CCC*, 1374). The risen Christ is present to his Church in many ways, but most especially through the sacrament of his Body and Blood in the Eucharist.

One of the stipulations God gave the Hebrews was to *consume* the Passover Lamb (see Ex 12:7–11). The paschal lamb was not killed in order to be looked at but to be eaten, consumed. Jesus Christ has not been slain merely that we may talk about him or think about him but that we may feed upon him. This is what the earliest Christians did when they gathered together on the first day of the week, and it's what Catholics do each time we gather for Mass because Christ commanded us to do so.

As we continue our journey of faith, we realize that we can't do it alone. We need the support of a community, and we need the Body and Blood of Jesus, which will sustain us in a way similar to the manna sustaining the Jewish people in the desert. We will discover that the Eucharist is not a puzzle to be solved but a mystery to be savored.

By instituting the Eucharist, Jesus didn't simply eat the Last Supper and then accept his fate; he transformed his physical suffering and death into a spiritual sacrifice of life-giving love. The Eucharist is the mystery and revelation of God's love in action, in which you and I are privileged to participate. If you want Christ, if you desire communion with his Body, his Church, it's the Eucharist that you need.

PRAY

Jesus, my Lord and God, I am grateful for your sacrifice on the Cross and your continual gift to me in the Eucharist. I am not worthy to receive you, yet you come to me under the appearance of bread and wine. May your gift of self through the Eucharist nourish my journey of faith until I meet you face-to-face. May I, in turn, serve you totally, freely, and faithfully. May my service bear fruit in the lives of others. Amen.

CONTEMPLATE

"The entire Passion, death, and Resurrection of Jesus Christ isn't just a story we've heard about, or know of, but something we experience in the here and now. We witness it each time we celebrate the sacrifice of the Mass. The Holy Spirit still awakens our faith as these sacred words are proclaimed. The sacrifice of Calvary and the unfathomable joy of the empty tomb are made visible as Jesus Christ is made present, Body, Blood, Soul, and Divinity in the Eucharist."

Fr. Jim Chern

WONDER

1. How can you create moments to pause in your daily life and realize the significance (and gift!) of each encounter?
2. How do you calm your mind and focus your thoughts on Jesus as Mass begins?
3. How can you prepare yourself for proper reception of the Eucharist?

22

DO YOU SEE THIS WOMAN?

Luke 7:44

Imagine yourself in *The Godfather*, the Academy Award–winning movie depicting the Corleone crime family. Envision yourself seated around the table where you are an invited guest of Don Corleone himself. To your right, around the large oval table, is the "Godfather" and his wife; next to them are their three adult sons and some other extended family members, guests, and associates—members of the mafia. Could you imagine one of the guests standing up with all eyes upon him, violently throwing his napkin on the table, and declaring in a loud voice: "This food is a disgrace! I wouldn't feed this to my dog!"?

What would be going through your mind at that point? If you are even mildly aware of the violent history and activities of this family you would be ducking under the table to avoid gunshots or, at the very least, you'd be thinking, "This is the last time I'll ever see that guy again. He's a dead man. He'll be sleeping with the fishes tonight."

Believe it or not, the mood Jesus created in the house of Simon the Pharisee could be likened to that created by the behavior of the man who insulted the Godfather in his own house, in the presence of his family and friends. No comparison in the words, mind you, but I *guarantee* you the feeling, the mood, and the reaction of those gathered were similar.

Jesus did not seem to have much concern for the cultural norms of his day if they superseded justice, mercy, and compassion. He was not afraid to speak the truth in love, tough love at that.

Do You See This Woman?

When Jesus was invited to Simon the Pharisee's house to dine, Simon intentionally omitted the required hospitality due any guest. One can speculate that this was done in order to show this young rabbi who was in charge and that, in order to speak, he should first be approved by the religious elite of the day. Hospitality also involves responsibilities on the part of guests. Rabbinic literature outlines many of these duties, including showing gratitude and not giving food to others without the host's consent. Just as the host is gracious, the guest is also obliged to be gracious. Whether an invitation to break bread is accepted or rejected, it carries social implications. Accepting an invitation to eat with someone speaks to trust. It also has to do with social status. A person of higher standing in the community can gift the host with his or her presence by agreeing to break bread together.

The social interplay that is going on in this story is often lost on our American ears but is very much at the forefront of this story. It's no wonder that the details are remembered and recorded by the early Christian community. Regardless of if you followed Jesus at that time, you would never have forgotten this particular meal, for the accepted protocols that were crossed and the etiquette that was ignored by Jesus were a slap in the face to the religious establishment of the time.

In this passage, found in Luke 7:36–47, before Jesus asks the question, a "sinful" woman enters the house where Jesus is dining and goes to Jesus' outstretched feet. She begins to bathe his feet with her tears, wipes them with her hair, kisses his feet, and pours out the ointment from her alabaster flask in order to anoint them. It was a costly, public demonstration of love. An alabaster flask of ointment points to her previous "sinful" life, which many speculate was prostitution. Her experience of Jesus' mercy and forgiveness leads her to "pour out" her old way of life at the feet of Jesus.

We hear the inner dialogue of Simon the Pharisee, who says to himself, "If this man were a prophet, he would know who and what sort of woman this is who is touching him, that she is a sinner." In Simon's mind, a prophet is one who avoids sinners; Jesus will reveal something greater, that in his prophetic role he not only has contact with sinners but intentionally offers love and forgiveness to them. Jesus speaks a parable concerning two creditors, one owing five hundred days' wages and another owing fifty. Both men had their debts forgiven because neither had the ability to repay. Jesus asks which of the two men will love the creditor more. Simon answers, "The one, I suppose, whose larger debt was forgiven." Then Jesus turns to the woman and says to Simon, "Do you see this woman? When I entered *your* house, *you* did not give me water for my feet, but she has bathed them with her tears and wiped them with her hair. *You* did not give me a kiss, but she has not ceased kissing my feet since the time I entered. *You* did not anoint my head with oil, but she anointed my feet with ointment. So I tell you, her many sins have been forgiven; hence, she has shown great love. But the one to whom little is forgiven, loves little."

I italicized the words "your" and "you" in the above verses because I think they rightly speak to Jesus taking a stand for this woman against the callous and unsympathetic perspective of Simon in his own home, in the company of his friends, which would have brought a great deal of shame to Simon.

Unfortunately, the name of Jesus has become synonymous with the words *nice, pleasant,* and *agreeable* in some circles. That's a shame. Do you really think they crucify nice people, pleasant people?

Becoming a disciple of Jesus means that we're becoming Christlike, not nice. Our measure of appropriate behavior must be in line with the Gospel and not according to whatever cultures and social situations we're in. More often than not, the problem is not that of being nice. The root cause of the problem is that many are weak and afraid of what others may think of them. This isn't a "nice" problem; it's a *fear* problem. Some people are so afraid of looking bad, mean, or selfish that they are conditioned to be "nice" or "pleasant" and put this ahead of doing the right thing at the expense of justice.

Following the way of Jesus also means having the wisdom to be introspective and the courage and fortitude to make changes where necessary. Are you too nice to yourself? When you ask yourself what behaviors hold you back from being like Jesus, you can adjust your behavior and the way you think for the better. When you allow others the space to give you the hard truths about yourself, without fear of repercussion, you'll get valuable perspective and make a giant leap forward in maturing as a Christian.

When we do follow the example of Jesus, we find that we become emotionally honest, which is healthy for everyone with whom we have contact. Yet few people want to be perceived as the "bad guy," the one who has to stop whatever's going on in order to speak up for justice, for those on the margins of society. It's easier to let these "inconveniences," these people, pass us by or to sweep them under the carpet. Christians are expected to make the tough decisions that serve the body of Christ and society's best interests, which demands a preferential option for the poor. Being "nice" is not the standard of a disciple of Jesus. Being anything less is lazy, irresponsible, and harmful to individuals and the Church.

PRAY

Lord Jesus, forgive me for those times I have sought the approval of others rather than being a person of justice and truth. Help me to stand up for the poor and those at the margins who don't have a voice in society. Like that nameless woman, may I pour out my former way of thinking about being nice at your feet. Thank you for leading the way by your witness and words. Strengthen me to do the same. Amen.

CONTEMPLATE

"To love God and neighbor is not something abstract but profoundly concrete: it means seeing in every person the face of the Lord to be served, to serve him concretely."

Pope Francis,
Address during Visit at the Homeless Shelter Dona Di Maria

WONDER

1. Have you always thought of Jesus as nice? How has that view changed in light of this story?
2. Is the root of the "nice" problem a fear to confront others?
3. Where are some areas in which God may be calling you to be a person of justice?
4. What do you need to "pour out" at Jesus' feet?

23

DO YOU REALIZE
WHAT I HAVE DONE FOR YOU?

John 13:12

As we continue down the road of discipleship and allow the Holy Spirit to transform us from within, we realize that there isn't a perfect program but there is a perfect person: Jesus Christ. This perfect person—who is one in being with the Father—continues to inspire and perfect us. St. Paul writes to the Colossians that Jesus is the visible image of the invisible God (see Col 1:15). St. John the Baptist simply says, "He must increase; I must decrease" (Jn 3:30). That's the goal of every follower of Jesus, to allow his presence to permeate every aspect of our lives so we hear, see, react, listen, and love like him.

Jesus gathers his apostles around the table and celebrates the Last Supper, which was a Passover meal. While the meal is significant for the institution of the Eucharist, Jesus will also model servant leadership for the twelve by washing his disciples' feet. St. John begins the second half of his gospel, often called the Book of Glory, with Jesus, towel around his waist, moving from one apostle to the next, washing their feet.

Do You Realize What I Have Done for You?

An example of what Jesus has done for us became real to me in an unexpected way while I was coaching varsity soccer at a high school. One of the players I had was a fine young man from Guatemala named Jorge. A short, stocky, and powerful centerfielder who could score from thirty yards out, he was a pretty normal teenager. When I first met him, I noticed some scarring on the left side of his face near his ear and neck that extended down below his shirt collar. His left arm had also been scarred, and his flesh had some twisted markings and discoloration from his wrist that extended to his shoulder. Every once in a while, after practice was over, Jorge would remove his shirt on his way to the locker room and reveal that this scarring affected the whole left side of his torso. It was jarring to see, mostly because it became obvious that this young man had suffered trauma in his young life.

When I knew Jorge, he was seventeen years old, and he had a little sister who was just seven. Now when you're seven, you have playdates after school and the occasional sleepover or half-sleepover where your friends stay until ten or eleven o'clock at night. Jorge found it odd that when he came home from school, his sister would quickly take her friends out of the room and go outside. This happened pretty consistently. A few times when her friends would stay late, she would give Jorge orders *not* to come into the family room while her friends were present. Jorge was perplexed. Here he was, ten years older than his sister, popular at school, and his sister didn't want him around her friends. Why?

Jorge confronted his sister about this behavior of avoiding him, and, after she shuffled her feet and avoided eye

contact for a moment or two, she fixed her gaze
older brother and pointed to his face and said, "Th
they're gross, disgusting; I don't want my friends to see
them!" Pretty harsh words to hear from your little sister.

Jorge was calm, cool, and collected and said to her, "We
need to talk." He then recalled the evening when he was
ten years old and she was a newborn living in their home in
Guatemala and how something awakened him in the middle
of the night. He walked outside his room, rubbing his eyes.
It must have been three or four in the morning. He made it
to the top of the stairs and looked down to see a small fire
that seemed to have started near an electrical outlet and that
grew bigger and bigger by the second as he watched, stunned
and speechless. Smoke quickly rose and filled the room and
being only ten years old, he ran down the stairs and exited
the house quickly.

He then looked at his sister, who was listening to his story,
and said, "Then I remembered you."

As quickly as he could, he ran back inside the house,
which was now engulfed in flames. He made his way up the
stairs while avoiding the staircase railing, which was ablaze.
The smoke was so thick that he could barely see anything
two feet in front of him, so using his hands, he felt his way
along the wall to his sister's room. He quickly wrapped her
in a blanket and cradled her in his right arm like a football. As
he exited the room, he again felt his way along the wall until
he got to the top of the stairs. The stairs were now totally
consumed in flames. He bent down to grab a quick breath
of air and proceeded down the stairs, all the while shielding
his sister from the flames. As he traveled a third of the way
down, he could feel the flames attacking his neck and smell

the unique stench of his hair burning while his pajama sleeve began to melt into his flesh. Halfway down the staircase, the intense heat was making his skin boil and he could feel it blistering, all the while shielding his sister from the flames. As his foot hit the floor at the bottom of the stairs, the agony was beginning to overwhelm him, but he made it to the front door with his left side seething in pain. He opened the door, staggered out a few steps and collapsed. It was in that fire that Jorge's parents were killed. A family from New Jersey later adopted Jorge and his sister.

When Jorge finished telling his sister the story, he pointed to his face and scars while saying, "When you see these scars, remember I have them because I love you; I didn't want to be separated from you."

His sister looked at him and then burst out crying. "I never knew; I never knew!" she sobbed and then threw herself into the strong embrace of her brother. She had seen those scars almost every day of her life, but she never knew what they meant. She never realized that they were the outward sign of her brother's love for her that he wore on his body each and every day.

Their relationship was forever changed. Such is the power of love. She was never ashamed of her brother or his scars again.

When we have been overwhelmed by the love of God through Jesus, when we realize that the scars he bears on his body are the outward sign of his love for us, we must respond. The only reasonable response to love is love. We express this love through having faith and trusting in the One who loves us and gave his life so that we might be reconciled to God. We express this faith by emulating the Master himself and serving others. We serve not because they are Catholic or Christian or because they even have faith. We serve because *we* have faith. They will know we are his disciples by our love for one another.

Every day we will be afforded opportunities to serve, opportunities to humble ourselves and "wash the feet" of others. St. Teresa of Calcutta said, "Do small things with great love. It's not how much we do but how much love we put into doing." Theological knowledge without loving service is not Christianity.

The Cross is God's principal act of love. Jesus' blood was shed for all, whether they know it or not, and yet a response is called for, a decision needs to be made when we internalize what God has done for us. We can begin by crying out, "Thank You, Lord!" and then we can live our lives responding to the love that has been shown to us.

PRAY

Lord Jesus, forgive me for those times when I thought more of myself than of others. May I serve with you by serving others in a spirit of charity and joy. Thank you for providing the model of love and sacrifice for me to follow. Amen.

CONTEMPLATE

"The cross is the school of love."

St. Maximilian Kolbe

WONDER

1. Have you encountered Jesus' love for you personally? How did you feel?

2. Have you ever verbally thanked God for Jesus' death on the Cross?
3. Who has modeled for you the sacrificial love displayed by Jesus?
4. In what ways can our whole lives be a response to the Cross of Jesus?

24

DO YOU LOVE ME?

John 21:16

"Do you love me?" Of all the questions to which we seek answers, this is really the only one that matters. With the assurance of love, we can survive anything. Without the assurance of love, no amount of money, power, or prestige will fill the void love's absence leaves.

I find it fascinating that it is Jesus who is asking this question of St. Peter. Peter, who was one of the first disciples; Peter, who is always named first among the apostles; Peter, who was one of Jesus' closest friends and witnessed Jesus transfigured before his eyes; Peter, "Cephas," the "Rock" about whom Jesus declared "upon this rock I will build my Church"; Peter, who denied he knew Jesus not once but three times and who ran off in fear after speaking boldly, "Even though I should have to die with you, I will not deny you" (Mt 26:35). It was Peter who abandoned Jesus at the Cross and allowed his friend, his Lord, to face crucifixion although Jesus had never abandoned him.

It should be *Peter*—on his knees, weeping, begging for the Lord's mercy and forgiveness—who asks, "Do you love me? . . . Lord, do you still love me despite my sin, despite my cowardice and lack of faith? Do you love me in my weakness and fear?" But no. It is Jesus who poses this question to Peter.

There are various motives to asking a question. Among them are to ascertain information, to test knowledge, and to seek assurance. Perhaps Jesus, in asking this question, allows Peter an opportunity to affirm and reestablish their relationship and even take it to a new level. There are clearly connections to be made with St. Peter's threefold denial and Jesus asking him the question three times.

In order to go a little bit deeper into what's being revealed in the pages of scripture, it is important to look at the original language in which the text was written. While the language that was spoken at the time was Aramaic, the New Testament is written in Greek, so the writers had to choose words that conveyed the original meaning.

In John 21:15, Jesus asks, "Simon, son of John, do you love me more than these?" In this passage, the Greek word used for love that Christ speaks of is *agape*. This is one of four Greek words used to communicate the one word "love" in English. In essence, Jesus asks Peter whether the love he has for him is not only greater than that of the others but whether this love is unconditional, if it is *agape* love.

This certainly is a profound question: *Do you not only love me more, but is your love boundless, unconditional, like my love for you?* Peter's response indicates the limitations of his humanity: "He said to him, 'Yes, Lord, you know that I love you.'" In Peter's response to Jesus' question, Peter chooses the Greek word *philio* for love. This word carries the connotation of affection and friendship, but Peter at this point is not *all in*. He loves Jesus but not unconditionally. He has lied to Jesus once about the extent of his love for him before the crucifixion, and he cannot do so again. At the very least, Peter is being honest, for the portrait of Peter we see is a humbled man, a man of broken and contrite spirit (see Ps 51:19). But Christ does not reject Peter's love even though it falls short of the question: "He said to him, 'Feed my lambs.'"

The second time Christ questions Peter, he again uses *agape*: "Simon, son of John, do you love me?" Once again Peter responds with *philio*, and once again Christ affirms the extent of Peter's commitment: "Tend my sheep." It appears evident that Christ would rather have a man love him honestly, if to a limited extent, than promise much, but not deliver (cf. Mt 26:33–35).

When Jesus questions Peter a third and last time, there is an added reason why Peter cries, for it is not only a reminder of his triple denial but the question Christ poses is amended, modified: "Simon, son of John, do you love me?"

Again, in English, there is nothing odd, but in the Greek the question is quite different. Christ no longer asks Peter for *agape* love, but rather, he asks Peter if his love is *philio*. Peter would have understood the importance of the variation in the questioning. Peter cries out not only because he has been questioned a third time but also because he understands that his love is limited and not as great as Christ's.

Peter can only reciprocate fully the love that Christ offers by giving up his life, yet he is not yet ready to do so. The greatest possession Peter has to offer, as with us, is his life. Peter replies, "Lord, you know everything; you know that I love you." Peter again uses *philio*, and for Christ, this admitted brokenness from a man who is desperate to love him with a human heart and all its failings is enough. Jesus responds, "Feed my sheep."

As Jesus asks St. Peter to feed his lambs and tend his sheep, we have the beautiful example of Jesus, the Good

Shepherd, who shepherds Peter. "Take my yoke upon you and learn from me, for I am meek and humble of heart; and you will find rest for yourselves. For my yoke is easy, and my burden light" (Mt 11:29–30).

Jesus does not force Peter to love him any more than he is capable of doing. Jesus meets him where he is and accepts the *philio* love he has for him. We will witness in the pages of Acts that after the Holy Spirit descends upon St. Peter and the Church, St. Peter will indeed continue his discipleship and follow Jesus and grow toward *agape* love. History will record the martyrdom of St. Peter, who did love Jesus with *agape* love as he gave his very life for Jesus in order to gain it eternally in heaven.

Do You Love Me?

It's still the most important question that's out there, and if we understand what Jesus is asking of us then we, like St. Peter, will realize that we are not there yet. We are indeed a work in progress cooperating with the Holy Spirit in order to allow Christ and his love to form us and work through us.

The first question in the pages of the Bible comes in the beginning, in the book of Genesis, where God asks a simple yet profound question: "Where are you?" This is not a directional question that God poses to Adam and Eve but a relational one. "Where are you in relationship to me, God?"

Where are you in relationship with Jesus? Do you love him on your terms or his? Are you *all in* and *committed* or a part-timer? Do you love him even when you don't understand him completely? Do you love him in good times and bad, or is your love for him dependent on how your day is going? Jesus loves us where we are, but he loves us too much to allow us to remain there. As followers of Jesus, this is a question that we have the opportunity to answer each day of our lives by how we live and by how we love one another.

PRAY

Jesus, thank you for loving me through it all and bringing me to this point in my life. Thank you for accepting St. Peter's *philio* love, for at times that's all I have as well. Yes, I love you. Help me to love you as you desire to be loved and to share that love with those I meet. Amen.

CONTEMPLATE

"Always be ready to give an explanation to anyone who asks you for a reason for your hope, but do it with gentleness and reverence, keeping your conscience clear, so that, when you are maligned, those who defame your good conduct in Christ may themselves be put to shame."

1 Peter 3:15–16

WONDER

1. Who has loved you with Christlike *agape* love?
2. What prevents us from giving Jesus our love in all things?
3. How can encountering Jesus in the sacraments and scripture increase our love?
4. How does our love for Jesus express itself in the world?

25

WHAT ARE YOU
DISCUSSING AS YOU WALK ALONG?

Luke 24:17

I was traveling to Green Bay, Wisconsin, to give a presentation, and the two-hour flight from Newark, New Jersey, to Chicago, Illinois, went pretty smoothly. The flight from Chicago to Green Bay was only about forty-five minutes, and the small airplane was packed except for one seat next to me. As the attendant was about to close the door, I was mildly excited that I might have a few extra inches of leg and arm room to stretch out. Wouldn't you know it that before the door closed, a voice could be heard yelling, "Wait! Wait!" as a disheveled-looking young woman in her mid-twenties, clothed in an old army jacket and sporting purple and green hair, thrust her arm in the opening just before the door was shut. I knew exactly where she was sitting.

I had the aisle seat as she made her way frantically toward her window seat in row eighteen, disrupting the settled passengers and unknowingly whacking each of them with her tattered backpack, which was slung loosely around her shoulder as she shuffled side-step down the aisle. I rose, anticipating her need to place the backpack in the overhead compartment and got whacked myself as she twirled around, trying to swing the backpack in front of her. I smiled and said, "No problem" as she moved into her window seat while I placed her backpack in the overhead compartment.

After I sat down and fastened my seatbelt, I turned and smiled at her and gave a slight head nod, saying, "You just made it." She smiled back, took a deep breath, and began talking for forty-two minutes straight. I swear, the young woman didn't take a breath. While I am known for my propensity to talk, I figured I'd just settle in and listen because she started out saying that she hadn't flown since she was five years old and she was so nervous and she was visiting her boyfriend in Wisconsin while her puppy is . . . I just let her go on and on and on.

As the flight attendant was making the final preparations for our landing, forty-two minutes later, the young woman finally took a breath and asked me, "So, what do you do?" I smiled and said, "Well, my name is Allan, and I work for the Catholic Church, and I—" Before I spoke another word, she stopped me and said, "Oh, I'm sorry; I don't believe in organized religion."

Now some people may have been offended by her statement, and after listening politely for forty-two minutes about her life, nodding and smiling at all the right places, I'm sure most people would cut me some slack if I expressed a little anger over her ill-mannered and disrespectful remark, cutting me off in mid-sentence, no less. However, without skipping a beat, my eyes lit up and a smile stretched my face as I looked right in her eyes and said joyfully, "Really, *you* should become Catholic; we're not that organized!"

I then gently expressed that I was genuinely sorry that she had a bad experience with organized religion and at the heart of the Catholic faith is Jesus, who is as alive today as he was when he appeared to Mary Magdalene and his disciples two thousand years ago. I smiled and said, "You know I'm going to pray for you." She smiled back and said, "Please do." I responded with, "How about right now?" She took my outstretched hand, and I said a short prayer for her as she spontaneously closed her eyes and, at the very least, had a caring stranger mention her name along with that of Jesus in a prayer.

Our God is certainly a God of surprises. Just when you think you have Jesus figured out or know what is going to happen next, God leads you in a different direction, much to your amazement and delight.

Jesus' final question that we'll cover models for us most perfectly how we are to act among others in sharing our faith. Yes, sharing our faith. Sharing with others our relationship with Jesus Christ. This phrase alone can be frightening for many because of their misunderstanding of what it means to share our faith. The word we use for sharing the faith is "evangelization."[17] Rather than shy away from this word, we should embrace it when we examine how Jesus models this for us. Fr. Thomas A. Judge remarked close to one hundred years ago that "In the ordinary providence of your everyday lives, you are the Church and you have the grace. You have the capacity and you are conditioned to make yourself responsible for the Catholic Church—at home in the street car coming and going to work, in your place of employment—where you are, there is the Church."

In the last chapter of Luke's gospel, we read that two of Jesus' disciples are going from Jerusalem to a village called Emmaus, which is seven miles from Jerusalem, seven miles from the other disciples. In essence they are going the wrong way, in the wrong direction. It is while they are heading away from Jerusalem that Jesus does two significant things. First, Jesus draws near to people going the wrong way. This is the beginning of evangelization: drawing near to people who are going the wrong way, who haven't allowed Jesus to be at the center of their lives. Jesus takes the initiative in drawing near, and then he does the second significant action: he engages them by asking questions.

Rather than berate these disciples for their unbelief and for leaving Jerusalem, Jesus calmly draws near and asks a couple of great questions. The first question reveals Jesus' humility: "What are you discussing as you walk along?" He is genuinely interested in what's important to them, and the question literally stops them in their tracks and opens them up to further conversation. As the passage continues, these two, on the road to Emmaus, talk about the things that have taken place in Jerusalem in recent days. Now nobody, and I mean nobody, knows better than Jesus the things that have happened in Jerusalem. Despite this fact, Jesus asks another question: "What things?" This question will allow Jesus to hear *their point of view* on the recent events concerning himself from their perspective.

A different perspective on evangelization, wouldn't you say? One that engages people where they are and listens to their point of view first.

Only after Jesus draws near and respectfully listens to them does he then share with them the Good News of God's plan. First Jesus takes them through the scripture, and they are so intrigued that they invite him, beg him, to stay with them, and he does.

This first part is a model for us in sharing the faith. What's our motivation for doing so? When we see a starving child on TV or read a news story where a family loses everything to a storm, our hearts are moved with compassion. Are not our hearts moved with that same compassion for those who don't know God, of God's love through Jesus, and the mercy, forgiveness, and new life that awaits us? We, too, are called to draw near, ask questions, listen, and then share our encounter with the risen Christ.

St. John Paul II said, "On her part, the Church addresses people with full respect for their freedom. Her mission does not restrict freedom but, rather, promotes it. *The Church proposes; she imposes nothing*" (*Redemptoris Missio*, 39). We don't desire nor should we attempt to "force" our beliefs on anyone; that's not the way of Jesus. We must, however, allow people the opportunity to embrace Christ, which occurs when we can propose who Christ is in our own lives. This encounter with Christ may come through both our words and our witness of a joy-filled life.

But it gets better!

Jesus doesn't just have a scripture study with the two disciples and leave. He stays, permanently! With the same two hands that were previously hammered into the wood of the Cross, "he took the bread, said the blessing, broke it, and gave it to them" (Lk 24:30). With that, their eyes were opened, and they recognized him. Jesus is recognized in the breaking of the bread, the Eucharist! Not only does Jesus share the scripture with them; he shares his very body with them under the appearance of bread, which his own pierced hands have broken. This is how Jesus remains present with us, not in some abstract way, not through some invisible cloud following us around, but in the Eucharist. The two disciples recognize this and quickly return to the community in Jerusalem, the other Body of Christ, the Church.

We have the privilege of sharing not only our encounter with Jesus but Jesus himself in the most Blessed Sacrament, the Eucharist, in which Jesus is fully present, body, blood, soul, and divinity and desires to become one with us.

What Are You Discussing As You Walk Along?

Those who have encountered Jesus are compelled to share their life-changing encounter with joy and to accompany others along the way to support and encourage them and to love them as brothers or sisters in Christ. In speaking to bishops from the United States in 1998, St. John Paul II put it this way: "The New Evangelization that can make the twenty-first century a springtime of the Gospel . . . will depend in a decisive way on the lay faithful being fully aware of their baptismal vocation and their responsibility for bringing the Good News of Jesus Christ to their culture and society."[18]

As you follow Jesus, you will have the opportunity to share him with others. It matters not your ability but rather your availability and willingness to speak up and name Jesus as Lord of your life.

PRAY

Lord Jesus, may I have the opportunity to share my faith with the same joy, ease, and enthusiasm that I have as I share so many other trivial events in my life. May the joy that comes from my relationship with you ignite a spirit that draws others to you as I articulate my encounter with you. Amen.

CONTEMPLATE

"As members of the Church, we preach the very person of Christ. Therefore, our efforts will succeed only when we ourselves have found the Lord himself. All evangelization presupposes that we are converted and that we are living an intimate and personal relationship with the Lord. What the world needs today are those who do not simply speak about Jesus, but those who make his truth real by the witness of their lives."

Bishop Arthur J. Serratelli, Bishop of Paterson, New Jersey

WONDER

1. What are the first words that come to mind when you hear the words "evangelization" or "sharing the faith"? Are they positive or negative?
2. Who has been a positive witness to Jesus in your life?
3. Have you ever heard a person give a dynamic testimony of their encounter with Jesus? What were your thoughts as you listened?
4. How can you intentionally draw near to those who don't know Christ?

CONCLUSION: RISE ABOVE

Contemplating the questions of Jesus provides food for thought and motivation for action. Regardless of where we are presently in our faith life, these questions continue to resonate within the human heart in order to move us forward in following Jesus Christ. As an institution, the Catholic Church from its inception honored men, women, and children and bestowed upon them the name of "saint" for their extraordinary lives and heroic virtue, which, for many, cost them their lives. This is what we strive for.

One question of Jesus that was not addressed in the preceding chapters was a question that Jesus posed to his mother: "Woman, how does your concern affect me? My hour has not yet come" (Jn 2:4). Mary's response is her last recorded words in scripture: "Do whatever he tells you."

The Catholic Church has always held Mary in high esteem for a multitude of reasons, but it comes down to one word. Mary said yes to God. That one yes set in motion the most mind-blowing event ever, that of God becoming man. The power of one person who says yes to God still has a rippling effect that has the power and ability to change the course of history. It can be said that human love attracts some, divine love attracts all. Mary was filled with this divine love. Perhaps just two thoughts regarding Mary as we look to her as both model disciple and Mother:

While on the Cross, Jesus looked down and said to John the Beloved, "Behold, your mother" (Jn 19:27). From that moment we are told the beloved disciple took Mary into his home. What a gift Jesus has given the Church and all disciples: the gift of his mother! A mother gives life physically and spiritually. A mother's love, like all love, extends across time and space, life and death. It nurtures, touches, soothes, and dwells in the heart even long after she's no longer physically present.

From the first moment a mother is aware of the new life within her, everything changes. A mother sees differently; she discerns, she worries, she reflects on the life within her, and she gives her life for her children as a continual act of self-denial and martyrdom. The eye contact, smell, verbal and non-verbal communication, and touch between a nursing mother and her child provide comfort and security after the first moments of birth. Mothers always want the best for their children, for such is the heart of a mother. We have such a mother, Mary, the Mother of Jesus, who desires the best for us and offers us her motherly affection as we follow her son.

Mary is also the perfect disciple, a model for us to emulate. Her last recorded words are simple, brief, and beautiful and were no doubt a model for Jesus growing up in the home with Joseph, his father: "Do whatever he tells you." These words spoken by Mary help us to cast our gaze on him who loves us and challenges us to rise above the expectations and pressures of our secular world and to live life in an extraordinary, supernatural way. Above all else, this means putting God at the center of our lives.

That is every disciple's task, to listen to Jesus' words and then to put them into practice as Mary did when she gave her yes to God at the annunciation and throughout her life. In following Jesus, may we seek her comfort and follow her example of faith, hope, love, and obedience to God. May we know her as our Mother, Mary, our Immaculate Queen of Peace.

NOTES

1. Gordon Franz, "Divine Healer: Jesus vs. Eshmun," *Archaeology and Biblical Research*, 2, no. 1 (Winter 1989): 24–28.

2. I have written a book on these encounters titled *Jesus in the House: Gospel Reflections on Christ's Presence in the Home* (Cincinnati: St. Anthony Messenger Press, 2007).

3. Gilbert Keith Chesterton, *Orthodoxy* (New York: John Lane Company, 1909), 29.

4. Jerome, *Commentariorum in Isaiam libri* xviii prol.: PL 24, 17B.

5. Gilbert Keith Chesterton, *What's Wrong with the World* (New York: Dodd, Mead, and Company, 1910), 48.

6. "John XXIII and Francis: What They Do, but Also How They Do It," *USCCB Blog*, accessed May 27, 2016, http://usccbmedia. blogspot.com/2013/10/john-xxiii-and-francis-what-they-do-but. html.

7. The phrase "chambers of the Sacred Heart" was spoken by a good friend, Fr. Tom Fallone, a priest in the Diocese of Paterson, NJ.

8. For more detailed information on the examen, visit http:// www.ignatianspirituality.com/ignatian-prayer/the-examen/ how-can-i-pray.

9. Catherine of Siena, *Dialogue on Providence*, chap. IV, 138.

10. St. Teresa of Calcutta thought it vital to have a contemplative branch of her order that focuses on the Mass, Eucharistic Adoration, prayer, and sacrifice.

11. *A Daily Thought from Sister Miriam Teresa* (Convent Station, NJ: Sister Miriam Teresa League, 1948).

12. John of the Cross, *Dark Night of the Soul*.

13. "Martyred with White Gloves," Morning Meditation by Pope Francis, June 30, 2014, accessed 27 May 2016, https://m.vatican.va/content/francescomobile/en/cotidie/2014/documents/

papa-francesco-cotidie_20140630_martyred-white-gloves.html.
The pope's words came as he celebrated Mass at the Casa Santa
Marta on the day in which the Church remembers the first Roman
martyrs who were martyred during Nero's persecution in AD 64.

14. Joachim Jeremias, *The Parables of Jesus* (Upper Saddle River,
NJ: Prentice Hall, 1963), 202.

15. Ibid.

16. Thérèse of Lisieux, *Letters of St. Thérèse to Her Sister Céline*,
Oct. 14, 1890.

17. I have written extensively about evangelization and how to
practically apply it in my book *Jesus the Evangelist: A Gospel Guide
to the New Evangelization* (Cincinnati: Franciscan Media, 2013).

18. John Paul II, in an address to the bishops of Minnesota,
North Dakota, and South Dakota on June 6, 1998, accessed 30
May 2016, https://w2.vatican.va/content/john-paul-ii/en/
speeches/1998/june/documents/hf_jp-ii_spe_19980606_ad-lim-
ina-usa-vii.html.

ALLAN F. WRIGHT is academic dean for evangelization at St. Paul Inside the Walls and an adjunct professor of biblical studies at Seton Hall University, where he received the "Many Are One" Servant Leadership Alumni Award in 2015.

He is a 1986 graduate of Seton Hall, earning a bachelor's degree in religious studies. He earned his master's degree in theology and biblical studies at Seton Hall, where he also received the Pope John Paul II Medal for Academic Excellence.

Wright is a speaker and the author of eight books, including *Daily Companion for Young Catholics* and *Jesus the Evangelist*. He received a first-place award in 2008 from the Catholic Press Association for *Jesus in the House* and was named teacher of the year in the Archdiocese of Newark in 2000. Wright is a member of the Knights of Columbus and the Missionary Cenacle Apostolate. He is the host of a weekly program on Radio Maria, *Jesus the Evangelist*. He is a frequent guest on Relevant Radio and EWTN and has been featured on Fox News and in *Catholic Digest* and the *National Catholic Register*.

He and his wife, Desiree, live with their four children in Basking Ridge, New Jersey.

AVE

Founded in 1865, Ave Maria Press,
a ministry of the Congregation of
Holy Cross, is a Catholic publishing
company that serves the spiritual and
formative needs of the Church and its
schools, institutions, and ministers;
Christian individuals and families; and
others seeking spiritual nourishment.

For a complete listing of titles from

Ave Maria Press

Sorin Books

Forest of Peace

Christian Classics

visit www.avemariapress.com

Ave Maria Press
Notre Dame, IN
A Ministry of the United States Province of Holy Cross